Gizzi's

KITCHEN
MAGIC

Gizzi's
KITCHEN
MAGIC
GIZZI ERSKINE

Virgin BOOKS

Published by Virgin Books 2010

2 4 6 8 10 9 7 5 3

Copyright © Gizzi Erskine 2010

First published in Great Britain in 2010 by
Virgin Books
Random House, 20 Vauxhall Bridge Road,
London SW1V 2SA

www.virginbooks.com
www.rbooks.co.uk

Addresses for companies within The Random House Group Limited
can be found at: www.randomhouse.co.uk/offices.htm

The Random House Group Limited Reg. No. 954009

A CIP catalogue record for this book
is available from the British Library

ISBN 9781905264643

The Random House Group Limited supports The Forest Stewardship Council [FSC],
the leading international forest certification organisation. All our titles that are printed
on Greenpeace-approved FSC-certified paper carry the FSC logo.
Our paper procurement policy can be found at www.rbooks.co.uk/environment

Photography © David Loftus

Printed and bound in Germany by Firmengruppe APPL, aprinta druck, Wemding, Germany.

FOR MY MAMA, MARIA, MY BIGGEST INSPIRATION.
AS YOU WILL SEE, THIS BOOK IS FULL OF ERSKINE SPECIALS.

Introduction viii

INTRODUCTION

I've been cooking for as long as I can remember but I always struggled with some basic techniques, which I knew I needed to have under my belt. When I was at catering school, I would become a wreck when we had a pastry-making class. Pastry was my cookery nemesis. The best pastry is short – crisp and a bit crumbly. The best short pastry is a bugger to roll out, it falls apart when you try to line a tart case and frankly made steam come out of my ears. But for years now I have been making my own pastry. I add more egg to it, that's all, which means I can work with it, and maybe if Michel Roux was coming for dinner I'd be exposed, but between me, you and your mates no one is going to know.

So, I decided I wanted to write a cookery book that would address some of the cookery problems I had faced, including how to make foolproof pastry. My book would have a back-to-basics approach. I wanted to write a book that would complement more advanced cookery books out there. One that would arm you with the techniques and core recipes that would make cooking your favourites easier. And so Gizzi's kitchen magic was born.

However, whilst this book includes techniques, tips and basic recipes, it is also full of inspirational recipes, which will help you practise some of these techniques, all with my own 'Gizzi' stamp on them. Some come from my travels around the world (grilled snapper with chilli and mango sauce, Vietnamese prawns and lemongrass, lamb massaman curry), some inspired by my favourite London restaurant dishes (black cod with plum miso, Afghan yoghurt chicken, chicken katsu curry), some Erskine classics (chicken in weeds, Parma ham and sage-wrapped veal with tomato and spaghetti), and some from my love of being a bit experimental (millionaire's shortbread with rosemary-infused salted caramel, Earl Grey chocolate fudge cake).

So bear with me on these techniques and hopefully they will allow you to approach cooking with more self-assurance. You'll be able to face the kitchen with new gusto and, fingers crossed, some of the magic that I have sprinkled into this book will translate into your own cookery.

Happy cooking!

Gizzi xx

KITCHEN BASICS

1

Where do you start when it comes to setting up a kitchen? It's hard to know, and it really depends on how much you think you're going to cook, but I hope you'll agree that having a fairly well-stocked kitchen is a good idea. You can bet your life that it's incredibly annoying to suddenly have the urge to bake cupcakes and not have any cupcake tins or cases to hand.

So, this chapter is all about kitchen basics, including what equipment you need to get started, what makes a great store cupboard, how to get the best out of a recipe, and how to chop an onion. I'm aware that some of you might be right up there with the Ramsays of the world and be perfectly adept at chopping an onion, but let me tell you, my mum – my biggest inspiration when it comes to food – is hopeless when handling a knife, which goes to show that even experienced cooks still have something to learn. I also hope that this book will reach a few novices and so I think it's important to start at the beginning.

★ ☆ Equipment ☆ ★

Most of us think 'basics' means only pans, knives and the odd spatula, but a well-equipped working kitchen has a lot more going for it than that. Here's my guide to what you should have and why. I know some of these can be expensive, but if you want to cook with conviction they're worth the investment.

PANS

Either stainless non-stick, cast iron or, if you're in a dream world (or mega-rich), copper. Get them in varying sizes, from a small milk pan (non-stick) right up to a huge stockpot. For a starter set I would advise going for a large heavy-based 20cm depth x 20cm diameter pan, a medium, 15cm depth x 15cm pan and a small 10cm deep x 12cm milk pan. Get two sizes of frying pan and go for non-stick. If you only want one, buy a larger pan. I live by my griddle pan. It's a fast and healthy way of cooking and adds heaps of flavour to dishes with the pretty lines it chars into the food. Make sure you get a cast iron one of these – the others are rubbish.

KNIVES

While it is so tempting to go for those starter sets of knives or for knives from a supermarket, I beg you – if you go out and spend money on one thing only, let it be knives. You don't need a huge set: just a large cook's knife, a small cook's knife, a fruit knife, a bread knife and a small paring knife. What makes a good knife is the quality of the metal. Japanese knives tend to be constructed in the same way as samurai swords, where the metal is folded over and over to ensure it's really strong (cool, eh?!). You can sharpen them yourself at home too, which is a definite benefit.

OTHER KITCHENALIA

* **A rolling pin:** Essential for making pastry dishes. For me the best pins are the same size all along – so no handles – but again, experiment to see what works best for you.

* **A pestle and mortar:** Great for pounding herbs or spices.

* **A palette knife:** For easing things up, spreading and a whole host of other things.

* **A fish slice:** For lifting things out of a pan.

* **A slotted spoon:** For scooping things out of liquid.

* **Wooden spoons:** For mixing and stirring.

* **A peeler:** For peeling vegetables. A very personal choice, but my favourite is the wide swivel peeler.

* **Hand whisks:** Get a big one for eggs and a small one for sauces, they are so useful.

* **Measuring spoons:** For accurate baking.

* **Chopping boards:** Wooden or plastic are fine but a solid wooden board tends to last longer.

* **Scales:** Electric ones are more accurate and easier to clean.

* **Measuring jugs:** Plastic or glass, these are essential for liquid quantities.

* **Baking sheets:** For biscuits or to put casseroles or ramekins on. Your kitchen can't be without them.

* **Roasting tin:** The more solid the better. The ones with handles are amazing (but expensive).

* **Cake tins:** An 22cm springform cake tin tends to cover all bases, although at least one 20cm sandwich tin is good to have around too.

* **A tart or pie tin:** You can't make a quiche or pie without one!

ELECTRICAL EQUIPMENT

* **Electric hand whisk:** If you have ever had to hand-whisk something, you will know why these are such a kitchen essential. They have so many uses and should be in every kitchen.

* **A blender/liquidizer:** You can buy hand-held versions of these that are excellent value, but they never quite make things smooth enough. Table-top blenders are fantastic for making really smooth soups, purées and sauces.

* **A food processor:** A great all-rounder. The only thing this does not do is whisk. You can get fantastic mini-processors which are great. You can liquidize in them but they will not get your food nearly as smooth as a blender would.

* **A table-top mixer:** On all cooks' wish lists and really helpful for mixing, kneading and whisking. Shallow as this sounds, they look fantastic too.

KNIFE SKILLS

* **To chop:** The correct way to chop is to draw the knife back and forth across the chopping board, from tip to base, without taking the knife off the surface, and feed the vegetable through your chopping motion with the back of your knuckles.

* **Chopping an onion**: Cut the onion in half from the pointy top down to the thick curly root. Trim the onion of its pointy top and curly bottom, then peel away the dry outer layers.Look at the onion – the bit where it clusters is the root. Slice into the onion in thin strips without cutting into the root. Cut the onion crossways, making sure you keep the distance between each slice the same. Repeat with the other side of the onion.

* **Chopping herbs:** Chop the herbs roughly first, then place one hand at the front of the blade and with a backwards/forwards motion chop the herbs into pieces. You can go as fine as you like here. At catering school we used to have to get parsley like dust – not fun, and pretty ugly if you ask me.

DIFFERENT VEGETABLE CUTS

* **Baton:** Cut the vegetable into a 5cm long cubed rectangle, then cut into 8mm strips, then cut each of these strips into batons.

* **Julienne:** Cut the vegetable into a 5cm long cubed rectangle, then cut into thin strips. Cut the strips lengthways into julienne matchsticks.

BASIC SKILLS

* **Dicing or chopping:** Cut your vegetable into cubes. A rough dice would be large cubes – great for potatoes. Medium dice would be around a 1cm cube, and small dice around a 5mm cube.

CRUSHING GARLIC

* Place an unpeeled garlic clove on your chopping board and slice off the root (the dry bit at the end). Lay the wide part of a large knife across it and push down so as to crush the garlic enough to release the skin, which you can now peel off.

* There are two ways to crush garlic. Either use a very fine microplane grater and grate the garlic into a purée, or chop the garlic into small pieces by rocking the knife back and forth over it until it is finely chopped. Sprinkle some salt over the garlic, then with the back of the knife press the pieces up and down to squash them into the salt.

☆ UNDERSTANDING A RECIPE ☆

The more experienced a cook you are, the more you will feel that cookery comes from somewhere within, but when you first start cooking it is worth looking at a recipe in the same way as you would an instruction manual. As with anything, the more you do it, the more confident you will get. Soon it becomes second nature and you will be putting your own flair and stamp on recipes. Here are a few pointers to think of when dissecting a recipe.

* Read through the recipe before you start working on it – that way you know exactly what to do before you do it.

* Work out in advance whether you want to work in metric (g/kg) or imperial (lb/oz) weights (assuming the recipe gives both) and stick to it. The youngsters among us will be going with metric, which is what I am using in this book.

* The same with oven temperatures – look at your oven dial. If it goes from around 100° to 280° it will be in Celsius, 300° to 600° will be Fahrenheit, and 1 to 8 will be the gas mark. If you have a fan oven you will need to decrease the temperature by 10°C/20°F or ½ gas mark.

* When baking, it is essential that you weigh all your ingredients accurately.

* Obvious, but easily done: don't leave any ingredient out!

* Always preheat your oven for at least 10 minutes before cooking. If you put something into a cold oven it will cook differently from how it will cook if you put it into one at the correct temperature. It can ruin baking and roasting dishes that you want to serve pink.

BASIC SKILLS

* Consider investing in some proper teaspoon and tablespoon measures. I know from my cutlery drawer that spoons come in all shapes and sizes, and at times cookery is such an accurate science that you're better off being precise.

* Get everything ready in advance. Pretend you're on your own cookery show and get it prepped – that way you will be sure nothing goes in at the wrong time and it will all be cooked as it should.

* When baking, make sure you use the right size tin.

THE PERFECT STORE CUPBOARD

What I often hear when people find out I'm a food writer is that they don't feel comfortable using cookbooks because they never have all the ingredients to hand. While I know that in some cases there are specific things you need to buy fresh, a well-stocked store cupboard will help you make this problem a thing of a past. The other great thing is that on those days when you think you have no food, your perfect store cupboard means you will be able to make something out of nothing.

Here's my guide to the ultimate store cupboard, but you can always start small and build up, the more confident you become. An avid cook tends to pick things up as they go anyway.

Tins
Chopped tomatoes
Chickpeas
Red kidney beans
Tuna in oil

Jars
Anchovies
Capers (I prefer them
   in vinegar)
Gherkins or cornichons
Tomato purée
White miso paste

Bottles
Kikkoman soy sauce
Thai fish sauce
Oyster sauce
Red wine vinegar
Cider vinegar
Sherry vinegar
Rice wine vinegar
Olive oil
Extra virgin olive oil
Corn or vegetable oil
English mustard
Dijon mustard

Grains, flours & baking
Pasta and spaghetti
Basmati rice
Risotto rice
Plain flour
Self-raising flour
Strong flour
Baking powder
Bicarbonate of soda

Spices
Ground coriander
Ground cumin
Turmeric
Cinnamon
Crushed chillies
Smoked paprika
Paprika
Cayenne
Saffron

Sweet
Golden caster sugar
Brown sugar
Light muscovado
Icing sugar
Honey
75% dark chocolate

Dried goods
Stock cubes or powder
Dried mushrooms
Maldon sea salt
Whole black pepper

Fresh
Milk
Butter
Double cream
Eggs
Fresh stock
Garlic
Ginger
Chillies
Herbs
Lemons
Limes

2

SOUPS & SALADS

As common as our daily bread, soups and salads crop up regularly in most people's diets. They are a lunchtime favourite and a fantastic opportunity to get loads of vitamins into our diet, not to mention being low in fat. Soups are as much about texture as flavour, so have a think about what you can add to them – croutons, creams, oils, pasta and rice all have their place and make a humble soup into a meal in itself.

With salads, a wonderful dressing can change the most basic of leaves into something quite extraordinary. The modest iceberg lettuce can really come to life with a piquant and creamy dressing. Also, play around with temperature. I love it when a key element in a salad is warm – it makes it feel all the more filling.

These days, familiarity seems to have bred contempt and I find that wilted, soggy salads and dull, insipid soups are far too often the norm – something I'm aiming to address in this chapter!

★ ☆ SOUPS TIPS & TRICKS ☆ ★

So let's start with soups. For me, a great soup needs a good base flavour and that will come from using a decent stock. Now we all know that making your own stock from scratch is second to none, but to make the amount of stock needed on a weekly basis the average household would have to be running its kitchen as if it were a restaurant. Who has time for that?! This doesn't mean you need to go for the over-processed cubed variety (although I admit there are some OK stock cubes on the market), but if you can go that extra mile and invest in fresh stocks from the chiller cabinet you will have much better soups and sauces – fact!

★ Chop everything to a similar size so it all cooks at the same time.

★ A lot of the flavour in your soup comes from the stock, so use the best quality you can find or, if you have the time, make your own (see page 246).

★ Cook your onions slowly, as this will release the sugars in them and add heaps of flavour to your soups.

★ Purée your soup for at least 30 seconds to ensure it is totally blended and without lumps.

★ If using potatoes, don't over-blend them or the soup could become gluey.

★ When making a smooth soup make sure you sieve the soup for a refined, extra-smooth result.

SOUP SKILLS

★ When making a chunky soup, treat it a bit like a stew and cook it slowly in order for the flavours to marry and mellow.

★ Never allow a cream based soup to boil as it can split. Also when reheating any type of soup, do not bring it to the boil.

★ Add any crisp ingredients to the soup at the end of cooking so they don't become soft or soggy.

★ Let your soup finish cooking before you add your garnish.

★ Chunky or smooth? Most people view chunky, broth-like soups as the more rustic version, while smooth, blended soups – particularly if they have been sieved – are more refined. Both are popular these days.

☆ ACCOMPANIMENT IDEAS ☆

OLIVE OIL
You can drizzle it on hot soups or make olive oil ice cubes for cold soups. Use only the best olive oil when doing this, though.

CRISP CROUTONS
For me the only way to make croutons is to tear smallish chunks of bread made with olive oil such as ciabatta, drizzle with more olive oil, rub with a clove of garlic and scatter over some fresh rosemary and bake at 200°C/gas 6 for 20 minutes.

PESTO
To add some really intense flavour to Mediterranean soups, a swirl of basil works a treat.

CHEESE
A good grating of Parmesan can really bring another dimension to your soup, but play around with your favourite flavour combinations. Goat's cheese is a winner with pea soups, and Cheddar sings with onion soups.

CREAM
Be it a drizzle of double or single, or a dollop of soured cream or crème fraîche, cream has to be the most classic of accompaniments for soups. I would generally only add cream to blended soups.

DUMPLINGS OR MATZO BALLS
As far as I'm concerned, chicken noodle soup isn't quite right without proper matzo balls. A clever cheat is using some filled pasta and poaching it in the soup for the last few minutes of cooking. I think beef-filled dumplings work brilliantly with chicken-broth soups.

★ ☆ SALAD TIPS & TRICKS ☆ ★

The best salads are a combination of colours, textures and flavours. Think about what you're trying to achieve. If you're wanting an Asian vibe, you will get the right flavours and textures by using herbs like coriander, basil (preferably Thai basil) and mint in place of salad leaves, while something more British might benefit from a combination of crisp and soft salad leaves.

★ Make sure you prepare everything as you are going to use it; most salad ingredients don't last very well and need to be eaten as fresh as possible.

★ A great way to wash salad leaves and keep them crisp is to soak them in ice-cold water for 10 minutes before using.

★ Dry salad leaves by dabbing them gently with kitchen paper.

★ Make your dressing in advance.

SALAD SKILLS

★ If you have a warm component to your salad, make sure you leave it to rest a little before adding it to the other ingredients, or it could cause your crisp leaves to wilt.

★ Do not dress your salad until you are about to serve it.

★ Oil-based dressings can be made in advance and stored in the fridge for a week or two.

Glittering GOLDEN SALAD DRESSING

This is my mum's recipe and it's pretty close to the classic. It works with every salad under the sun. Keep it in a jam jar in the fridge for up to two weeks so you can be ready for salad-dressing action whenever you need it.

Makes 150ml
Preparation time 5 minutes

1 teaspoon Dijon mustard
1 tablespoon sherry vinegar
sea salt and freshly ground black pepper, to taste
a squeeze of lemon juice
½ teaspoon golden caster sugar
150ml really good-quality extra virgin olive oil

Put the mustard, vinegar, salt, pepper, lemon juice and sugar into a small bowl. Slowly whisk in the olive oil (using one of those mini sauce whisks if you have one) and continue to whisk until the dressing has emulsified slightly. Alternatively, put all the ingredients into a jam jar and shake until emulsified.

My Cheat's CAESAR SALAD DRESSING

The low-fat Caesar salad dressing I made in *Cook Yourself Thin* was probably one of my most successful recipes. I got so many emails about it, and people genuinely did think it was better than the real thing. You get all the flavour of the classic version but it's so much lighter, and a damn sight easier to make to boot. I have tweaked this version so that the emphasis is not quite so light but it's doubly delish!

Makes 150ml
Preparation time 5 minutes

1 small garlic clove, peeled and grated (with a fine grater or microplane)
2 anchovy fillets in olive oil, from a jar
30g Parmesan cheese, freshly grated (with a fine grater or microplane)
sea salt and white pepper, to taste
3 tablespoons Greek yoghurt
2 tablespoons extra virgin olive oil
a squeeze of lemon juice

Place the garlic, anchovies, Parmesan, salt and pepper in a mortar and pound to a smooth paste with a pestle. A tablespoon at a time, add the yoghurt, olive oil and lemon juice until combined and season again to taste.

SEX IT UP!

VINEGARS

Whether you use red wine, white wine, cider, sherry or balsamic vinegar, they all work brilliantly in salad dressings, each one bringing it's own flavour. Or you could use one of the flavoured vinegars. Tarragon vinegar always adds a different dimension to salads.

CITRUS

Lemon, lime, grapefruit, clementine and orange juices are all delicious in dressings. Add the zest as well, for extra zing.

OILS

Using unusual oils is another way to add pizzazz to a dressing. Nut oils are fabulous, and a dash of toasted sesame oil is brilliant for an Asian flavour. Make sure you dilute really strong oils with extra virgin olive oil.

AROMATICS

Add herbs, spices or garlic to flavour your dressing. Be quite frugal with these, as too much will overpower the dish.

SWEETNESS

Honey, maple syrup and brown sugar are great ways to add sweetness to a dressing.

Mexican chicken
TORTILLA *soup*

If you go to any street market in Mexico they will be selling a variation on this soup. It is actually a cleansing broth with a hot-and-sour note, filled with chunky chicken and sweetcorn and topped with creamy avocado and swirls of crisp tortilla. The tortillas act like croutons and stay crisp on top but soak up all the lip-smacking juices underneath.

Serves 4
Preparation time 15 minutes
Cooking time 35 minutes

3 tablespoons olive oil
2 onions, peeled and finely chopped
4 garlic cloves, peeled and finely chopped
2 red or green chillies, seeded and chopped
3 ripe tomatoes, chopped
850ml chicken stock
1 x 285g tin of sweetcorn, drained
2 whole chicken breasts, skinned
sea salt and freshly ground black pepper

For the topping
2 medium (20cm) flour tortillas, cut in half, then thinly sliced
1 avocado, chopped
a handful of fresh coriander leaves, to serve

Heat 2 tablespoons of oil in a large pan. Add the onions and fry over a low heat for 10 minutes or until they have softened and started to turn a golden colour. For the last minute, add the garlic and chillies. Throw in the tomatoes, then pour over the stock. Add the sweetcorn and chicken and simmer slowly for 15 minutes. Remove the chicken breast and put to one side, and cook the soup for a further 10 minutes. Then season to taste.

Shred the chicken and return it to the pan, along with any juices. Heat the remaining tablespoon of oil in a frying pan. Toss in the tortilla strips and fry for 3 minutes, or until crisp and golden. Ladle the soup into bowls and top with a sprinkling of tortillas, some avocado and coriander.

CHEAT

For an even speedier soup, why not add tortilla chips instead of using flour tortillas?

Posh TOMATO SOUP
with cappelletti

Smoked tomatoes may not be widely available, but you should be able to find them at farmers' markets. If you can't, use the same quantity of sunblush tomatoes mixed with 1 teaspoon of smoked paprika. Cappelletti are simply tiny filled pasta, similar to tortellini, but if you can't find them use whatever small stuffed pasta you like.

Preheat the oven to 200°C/gas 6. Lay the pepper halves, cut side up, on a baking sheet and top with the vine tomato halves. Drizzle with 1 tablespoon of olive oil and season with salt and pepper. Whack the baking sheet into the oven and roast for 25 minutes, or until the peppers and tomatoes are starting to blacken and have softened.

Meanwhile, put the other tablespoon of oil into a small pan. Throw in the onions and fry over a fairly low heat for 10 minutes, so that they become really softened and start to caramelise and sweeten. For the last minute of the cooking time, add the garlic.

When the peppers and tomatoes are done, put them into a blender with the onions, garlic, smoked tomatoes, vegetable stock and basil sprigs. Process for 2 minutes, until smooth, then return the soup to the pan (for a really smooth consistency, sieve it from the blender into the pan) and reheat really gently. Meanwhile, bring a pan of salted water to the boil. Add the cappelletti and boil for 1–2 minutes, then drain.

Ladle the soup into bowls and top each serving with some of the cappelletti, a drizzle of pesto and a grating of Parmesan.

Serves 4 as a starter or 2 as a main course
Preparation time 10 minutes
Cooking time 35 minutes

3 red peppers, seeded and halved
5 vine tomatoes, halved
2 tablespoons olive oil
sea salt and freshly ground black pepper
1 onion, peeled and finely chopped
3 garlic cloves, peeled and finely chopped
½ tub or 100g oak-smoked tomatoes, or the same quantity of sunblush tomatoes mixed with 1 teaspoon smoked paprika
200ml vegetable stock
3 sprigs of fresh basil
100g cappelletti of your choice (I love the goat's cheese ones)
pesto, to drizzle
Parmesan cheese, to serve

Gazpacho WITH KING PRAWNS & *quails' eggs*

A gazpacho has all the components of a salad, even down to the dressing and the croutons, whizzed together to emulsify and create a tangy soup that screams 'summer'. On its own it's brilliant – with prawns and quails' eggs it turns into a dish that will wow anyone. If, like me, you sometimes find yourself inundated with tomatoes and never know what to do with them all, look no further.

Place the tomatoes, cucumber, red pepper, chilli, garlic, bread, basil sprig, olive oil, sherry vinegar, sugar, salt and pepper in a mixing bowl and stir together as if you're making a salad. Place half this mixture in a blender and blitz for 1 minute, or until smooth. Push the soup through a fine sieve into another mixing bowl. Repeat with the other half of the 'salad'.

Check the seasoning and place in the fridge for an hour. You can eat the soup immediately but it does benefit from a bit of chilling time! While it's chilling, hard-boil your quail's eggs in a pan of boiling water for 7 minutes.

When you're ready to serve the gazpacho, ladle it into bowls. Top each bowl with some of the chopped vegetables, 3 king prawns and 3 halves of quails' egg, and drizzle with extra virgin olive oil.

Serves 4
Preparation time 20 minutes
Cooling time 1 hour

1kg vine-ripened tomatoes, skinned if you can be bothered
½ cucumber, peeled and chopped
1 red pepper, seeded and chopped
1 red chilli
3 garlic cloves, peeled
100g good-quality white bread, crusts removed, soaked in water
1 sprig of fresh basil
100ml extra virgin olive oil, plus extra for drizzling
2 tablespoons sherry vinegar
1 teaspoon golden caster sugar
sea salt and freshly ground black pepper, to taste

To serve
1 tomato, seeded and chopped
¼ cucumber, seeded and chopped
¼ red pepper, chopped
12 cooked king prawns, peeled
6 hard-boiled quails' eggs, peeled and halved

Chicken satay NOODLE SOUP

I am an Asian food freak, and I make it pretty much on a daily basis. It's so fast to cook and fresh, which are both things people are often desperate to achieve. Asian food is all about the preparation. So I set out to create a recipe where speed and simplicity are the priorities. I have used a ready-made yellow curry paste and that is totally fine – you would be surprised at how many Thai restaurants use the pre-prepared stuff, even in Thailand. The soup is served with the classic satay accompaniments – cucumber, spring onions, chilli, peanuts and coriander – with all those flavours you would never know you could make this in half an hour! It will become a week-night staple – you'll see.

Serves 4
Preparation time 10 minutes
Cooking time 20 minutes

4 boned chicken thighs
1 teaspoon ground coriander
½ teaspoon turmeric
½ teaspoon crushed dried chillies
1 teaspoon sea salt
1 tablespoon olive oil
1 x 400g tin of coconut milk
400g chicken stock
2½ tablespoons yellow curry paste
1 tablespoon smooth peanut butter
2 tablespoons Thai fish sauce
2 tablespoons brown sugar
juice of ½ lemon
1 tablespoon chilli oil
sea salt and freshly ground black pepper
250g thin or wide rice noodles

To serve
a small bunch of fresh coriander, leaves picked
a small bunch of fresh mint, leaves picked
¼ cucumber, sliced
2 spring onions, sliced
2 handfuls of beansprouts
1 red chilli, sliced
a large handful of roasted peanuts or cashews, chopped

Rub the chicken thighs with the coriander, turmeric, dried chillies and salt. Heat the oil in a frying pan, put the thighs in skin side down and fry for 10 minutes over a lowish heat or until the skin is crispy. Turn them over and cook for a further 6 minutes. Set the pan aside and let the chicken rest skin side up in the pan.

Put the coconut milk, stock, curry paste, peanut butter, fish sauce, brown sugar, lemon juice and chilli oil into a pan and heat until the sugar has melted. Raise the heat, bring to the boil, and cook for 5 minutes. Season to taste.

Cook the rice noodles according to the packet instructions and divide between 4 bowls. Ladle the soup into the bowls, then top each serving with some coriander, mint, cucumber, spring onions, beansprouts, chilli and nuts. Slice the chicken thighs and distribute between the bowls. Serve piping hot.

Pink soup WITH SOURED CREAM & *chives*

I don't know if it's a girly thing, but for me any food that has such a vibrant colour has got to be good for the soul. This soup lies somewhere between that Polish staple, borscht, and a delicious side dish my mother (who's part Polish) makes with red cabbage and apples. All the ingredients have big flavours, so it's not for the faint-hearted!

Heat the oil in a large, heavy-based pan. Add the onion, beetroot, cabbage and apples and cover with a lid. Sweat the vegetables over a low heat for 20 minutes, stirring every so often, until the veggies have softened, but make sure they do not have too much colour.

Stir in the sugar, vinegar, dried chillies, allspice, cloves and bay leaves and add the stock. Let it bubble away for 10 minutes, then turn off the heat. Remove the bay leaves and whiz the soup in batches in the blender. Pour the blended soup back into the pan through a sieve. Season to taste.

To serve, ladle the soup into bowls and top each serving with a tablespoon of soured cream and some snipped chives.

Serves 4
Preparation time 20 minutes
Cooking time 30 minutes

2 tablespoons olive oil
1 onion, peeled and chopped
4 raw red beetroot, chopped (no need to peel)
½ red cabbage, chopped
2 red apples, cored and chopped (no need to peel)
2 tablespoons brown sugar
2 tablespoons red wine vinegar
½ teaspoon crushed dried chillies
½ teaspoon allspice
pinch of ground cloves
2 bay leaves
1.5 litres beef or vegetable stock
sea salt and freshly ground black pepper
4 tablespoons soured cream, to serve
finely chopped chives, to garnish

SEX IT UP!

Chilled pink soup: For a summery variation, chill the soup and serve with soured cream and ice cubes frozen with some chopped chives in them.

Chinese chicken & MUSHROOM SOUP *with* SESAME PRAWN TOAST CROUTONS

You don't get much more British than chicken and mushroom soup … unless of course you cook the chicken and mushrooms with an aromatic broth of ginger, soy and sesame and add heat in the form of crisp, fresh red chillies. Purists will say that prawn toasts are not croutons, but they are great for dunking into soup and they give you the feeling of bringing a Chinese takeaway home with you.

Serves 4
Preparation time 20 minutes
Cooking time 20 minutes

4 tablespoons olive oil
5cm piece of fresh root ginger, peeled
   and sliced
3 garlic cloves, peeled and crushed
2 boneless chicken breasts, each cut into
   15–20 chunks
20 shiitake mushrooms, halved or quartered,
   depending on size
1 litre hot chicken stock
1 tablespoon soy sauce
1 teaspoon sesame oil
1 rounded tablespoon cornflour

For the 'croutons'
8 raw king prawns, peeled
a pinch of sea salt
1 free-range or organic egg white
1 tablespoon double cream
a generous squeeze of lemon juice
a pinch of nutmeg
1 small skinny white baguette, sliced on
   the diagonal into 8 slices
sesame seeds

To serve
4 spring onions, chopped
1 red chilli, deseeded and thinly sliced

Heat 1 tablespoon of olive oil in a large, heavy-based pan. Add the ginger and garlic and stir-fry for 1 minute, or until they start to take on some colour. Throw in the chicken and mushrooms and stir-fry for a further 5 minutes, or until lightly golden.

Cover with the hot stock, then lower the heat to a simmer. Add the soy sauce and sesame oil. In a separate bowl mix 5 tablespoons of the hot liquid with the cornflour. This will become paste-like; you may need to add more stock to make it a little runny. Pour it into the soup, stirring as you go. After a few minutes, the soup will begin to thicken. Leave it to simmer away for 10 minutes.

Meanwhile, make the sesame prawn toast croutons. Place the prawns, salt, egg white, cream, lemon juice and nutmeg in a food processor and pulse every so often until you have a chunky purée. Spread this in a thick layer on the slices of bread, then coat the purée with the sesame seeds. Heat the remaining 3 tablespoons of olive oil in a frying pan, add the toasts – sesame seed side down – and fry for a few minutes on each side, or until the sesame seeds are toasted and the bread is crisp and golden. Drain on kitchen paper.

Add the spring onions to the soup for the last minute of cooking, then ladle into bowls. Top with the sliced chillies and serve each bowl with 2 sesame prawn toasts.

Smoked ham & PICCALILLI SALAD

I love piccalilli and really wanted to find a way to put it into a salad, but, alas, it doesn't seem to work – it's all a bit too gungy. So instead I decided to make a salad with crunchy peppery vegetables and drizzle it with a fantastic, fragrant, light, bright yellow dressing. With strips of smoked ham laced through it, this makes a marvellous salad.

Bring a pan of salted water to the boil and throw in the cauliflower and beans. Boil for 2 minutes, then drain and plunge immediately into iced water to cool and stop the cooking process. When they have cooled, drain and place in a mixing bowl with the radishes, carrots, onion and gherkins.

To make the dressing, place all the ingredients in a clean jam jar, pop the lid on tightly and shake the jar like crazy for 30 seconds.

Pour half the dressing over the crunchy vegetables and mix thoroughly. Lay the chicory and Little Gem lettuce leaves on a large plate and drizzle with the rest of the dressing. Top with the crunchy vegetables and torn ham and serve immediately.

Serves 4
Preparation time 20 minutes

½ cauliflower, broken into florets
30 green beans, trimmed
2 radishes, thinly sliced
2 carrots, thinly sliced
½ red onion, peeled and thinly sliced
2 gherkins, thinly sliced
1 head of chicory, leaves separated, washed and dried
1 head of Little Gem lettuce, leaves separated, washed and dried
200g smoked ham, preferably torn from a ham hock, or thickly sliced ham, torn into pieces

For the dressing
1 teaspoon English mustard powder
½ teaspoon ground turmeric
a pinch of allspice
a grating of nutmeg
½ garlic clove, peeled and grated
½ teaspoon sugar
sea salt and freshly ground black pepper
2 tablespoons cider vinegar
3 tablespoons extra virgin olive oil

Japanese rare ROAST BEEF SALAD WITH mixed radishes

This recipe is based on Japanese beef tataki, a simple seared beef dish. Most of the ingredients are fairly easy to find, but it may take a trip to Chinatown to track down daikon radish. The beef, peppery watercress, radishes, ginger and wasabi dressing all combine to create a flavourful party on your plate.

Heat the oil in a frying pan until really hot. Season the steaks with salt and pepper and sear them for 20 seconds on each side – the meat should be fairly dark on the outside and still really rare in the middle. Remove from the pan and leave to rest for 1 hour in the freezer until the meat firms up and is almost frozen (a restaurant trick that will make it easier to slice). Technically you need to let things cool before popping them into the fridge or freezer, but as this meat has simply been seared it should not be too warm. Use your own instincts though – if you think it needs to cool a little before freezing, feel free to let it do so.

Mix the ginger, soy sauce, rice wine vinegar and wasabi paste in a small bowl. When you're ready to serve, remove the beef from the freezer and slice thinly, aiming to cut 12 slices from each steak. (You can sneak the end bits as a chef's perk!) Lay 6 slices, overlapping each other, on each plate. Top with the watercress, tomatoes, a sprinkling of daikon radish, red radishes and spring onion, and pour over the soy and wasabi sauce. Finally sprinkle with sesame seeds and chives to serve.

Serves 4
Preparation time 10 minutes
Cooking time 2 minutes
Cooling time 1 hour

1 tablespoon olive oil
2 beef fillet steaks, each 5cm thick
sea salt and white pepper
a 3cm piece of fresh root ginger, peeled and grated
2 tablespoons Kikkoman soy sauce
2 tablespoons rice wine vinegar
1 teaspoon wasabi paste
1 bunch of watercress, trimmed
8 cherry tomatoes, preferably a mixture of red and yellow
5cm piece white daikon radish (or 8 normal white radishes), peeled and sliced into thin matchsticks
8 red radishes, quartered
2 spring onions, thinly sliced
black and white sesame seeds, for sprinkling
4 chives, each snipped into 4 pieces

WHY NOT TRY? Make a seared tuna salad by replacing the beef with 2 tuna steaks.

Sticky THAI CHICKEN & *mango salad*

If we were in Thailand we would be eating this salad with firm, under-ripe, mouth-puckering green mangoes, but the crispy chicken also sings alongside creamy, juicy ripe ones. It's sweet, it's sticky, it's sour, it's hot, it's refreshing – so although it may not be completely authentic, there is no denying that this salad's jolly good.

Serves 4
Preparation time 20 minutes
Cooking time 15 minutes

1 tablespoon olive oil
4 boneless chicken thighs, skin left on
sea salt and freshly ground black pepper
3 tablespoons Thai fish sauce
3 tablespoons golden caster sugar
1 tablespoon lime juice
a 3cm piece of fresh root ginger, peeled and
  grated
1 red Thai chilli, chopped

For the salad
2 tablespoons olive oil
8 banana shallots, peeled and sliced
1 ripe but firm mango
2 red chillies, seeded and cut into thin strips
a small bunch of fresh coriander, leaves picked
a small bunch of fresh mint, leaves picked
juice of 2 limes
2 tablespoons Thai fish sauce
1 teaspoon caster sugar

WHY NOT TRY ?

Sticky Thai chicken & pomelo salad:
A pomelo, which is like a giant grapefruit, would make a fantastic alternative to mango in this salad. Simply swap the mango for ½ a pomelo, peeled and segmented.

Heat the oil in a frying pan. Rub the chicken thighs with salt and pepper and lay them skin side down in the pan. Cook over a medium to low heat for 6–8 minutes, then turn them over and repeat on the other side until they are cooked through and the skin is crisp and golden.

Remove the chicken from the pan and set aside while you make the glaze. Add the fish sauce, sugar, 1 tablespoon of lime juice, the ginger and chilli to the pan and stir until the sugar has melted. Let the sauce bubble for a few seconds, then return the chicken thighs to the pan briefly and coat them in the sauce. Remove from the heat and leave to rest while you make the salad.

Heat the oil in a smaller frying pan and add two-thirds of the shallots. Stir-fry them over a medium to high heat for 5 minutes or until crisp and golden, then turn them out on to a sheet of kitchen paper to cool and drain.

Peel the mango, then slice each of the cheeks off. Slice the mango flesh into long, thin slivers and put them into a bowl with the remaining uncooked shallots, red chilli and herbs. In a smaller bowl, mix together the lime juice, fish sauce and sugar, and pour over the salad. Toss the salad and divide it between 4 plates.

Slice the chicken and put a few slices on each plate. Sprinkle with some of the crispy shallots, then drizzle the remaining sauce in the pan over the chicken and serve.

Roasted aubergine, mint
& YOGHURT SALAD

This dish came about by accident! We were filming on location and had loads of barbecued aubergine, so I wanted to make something with it. After a rummage in the fridge I came up with this recipe, and it's addictive. Stuff it into pitta bread or serve it with roast lamb – either way, it's pretty fantastic.

Serves 4
Preparation time 10 minutes
Cooking time 30 minutes
Cooling time 15 minutes

2 aubergines, halved
1 garlic bulb
8 tablespoons extra virgin olive oil
sea salt and freshly ground black pepper
juice of ½ lemon
250g Greek yoghurt
a small bunch of fresh coriander, chopped
a small bunch of fresh mint, chopped

Preheat the oven to 200°C/gas 6. Lay the aubergines, cut side up, and the garlic bulb on a baking tray, and rub them with 4 tablespoons of olive oil. Season with salt and pepper. Place in the oven and bake for 30 minutes, or until the aubergine is starting to char and the garlic is soft.

Leave to cool for 15 minutes, then carefully cut the garlic bulb in half and squeeze the soft inside on to a chopping board. With the back of a knife, squash the garlic until it forms a paste. Place the aubergines on the same chopping board, remove and discard the stalks, then chop the flesh into small chunks until it resembles a chopped salad. Drizzle with a good 2 tablespoons of olive oil and add the lemon juice.

Spread the yoghurt on a serving plate and top with the aubergine salad. Scatter over the fresh herbs and drizzle with a good lug of olive oil before serving.

Pan-fried HALLOUMI with BLACK BEAN, AVOCADO & CHILLI SALSA

Classically, halloumi cheese is served with Cypriot or Turkish accompaniments, but it works well with any strong flavours. Here I have used classic Mexican ingredients, one of the key components being chipotle chillies, which are smoked, dried jalapeños. They have such a distinct smoky flavour and will be a revelation to chilli fans.

Rub the halloumi slices with olive oil and lay them in a hot pan. Pan-fry for 2 minutes on each side, until golden-brown, then remove to a large serving platter.

In a mixing bowl, combine the remaining ingredients to make the salsa. Check the seasoning, and spoon it over the halloumi. Serve immediately.

CHEAT If you can't find chipotle chillies you may be able to find chipotle chilli Tabasco in your local supermarket; failing that, a nice fat fresh red chilli will do the job.

Serves 4
Preparation time 10 minutes
Cooking time 5 minutes

2 x 200g packs of halloumi cheese, each cut into 10 slices
1 tablespoon olive oil

For the salsa
200g tinned black-eyed beans, drained and rinsed
1 large ripe but firm avocado, peeled and chopped
1 large vine tomato, seeded and chopped
2 spring onions, chopped
1 chipotle chilli, soaked overnight in boiling water, then drained and chopped
1 garlic clove, peeled and grated
½ teaspoon ground cumin
juice of 1 lime
1 tablespoon extra virgin olive oil
sea salt and freshly ground black pepper

EGGS

Superfoods may be all the rage at the moment, but there's one food that has been super for centuries: the humble egg! As well as being nutritionally valuable – containing protein, vitamins and minerals – eggs are the most flexible food known to man. Eaten boiled, poached, fried, scrambled, as an omelette, baked or souffléd, eggs are also used to bind, emulsify, bake and glaze. What's more, they couldn't be easier to get to grips with. For me, that takes them beyond the realm of a superfood and propels them to godly status.

That being said, egg cookery is quite a skill, and as the legend that is Delia Smith taught us, sometimes learning to cook comes from the simple things like knowing how to boil an egg. I've met chefs who have small breakdowns when asked to poach eggs, and it's quite normal to get all panicky when coming to the end of scrambling eggs, when you don't want them to go too far, but you're still questioning whether or not they are too runny.

The thing about eggs is that there has to be a bit of bravado included when cooking with them. The more you work with them the more confident you will get, so throw yourself in there, it's not that hard. It's only an egg, after all.

★ ☆ TIPS & TRICKS ☆ ★

Many people don't know how to determine whether an egg is fresh or not, but it's as easy as pie. Fill a glass or bowl with cold water and carefully lower your egg into it. If the egg sinks, it is fresh; if it starts to rise to the top it is off – as an egg ages, it fills with gas, which causes it to rise or float in water. Needless to say, the fresher your egg is the better it will taste – and freshly laid eggs are quite a fantastic experience if you have never had them before.

HOW BIG IS MY EGG?

You will tend to find that in most cookbooks they suggest you use large eggs, and all my recipes are the same. Eggs come in various sizes, so if you're simply poaching, scrambling or frying your egg, go for whichever size you like. However, when it comes to baking, I wouldn't risk messing around with egg sizes.

FACTORY FARMED? FREE-RANGE? ORGANIC?

When we are talking about animal welfare there is no option but to choose free-range eggs. Organic are even better, as they are free from antibiotics and the food the bird has eaten is free of pesticides, which naturally is better for you, but I do know they are quite a bit more expensive. Go for whatever you can afford, but do the poor chickens a favour and don't condone factory farming.

HOW DO I STORE MY EGG?

Eggs can be stored in or out of the fridge, but a refrigerated egg has a longer life. The only down-side to this is that most recipes require room-temperature eggs, so just remember that you must remove the eggs from the fridge about an hour before using them.

CRACKING AND SEPARATING EGGS

Hit your egg firmly but not too hard at the widest part to break it, then, over a container, use both hands to separate the eggshell. It should break easily. If you need a whole egg, simply tip it into a container. If you need to separate the egg white from the yolk, allow the white of the egg to fall into the container while tipping the yolk gently between the halves of the shell until there is no more egg white left. Tip the egg yolk into a separate container. Be really gentle when doing this so that you do not break the yolk.

EGGS

Cooking Eggs

BOILED EGGS

* If your eggs are straight from the fridge or really fresh (laid that day), they may need about 30 seconds longer boiling time.

* Carefully lower the eggs into the boiling water with a spoon.

* Do use a stop watch or time your eggs carefully if you want them to be perfectly cooked.

* Peeling an egg under running water while still slightly warm will ensure that the shell peels off really easily.

OMELETTES

* Always cook omelettes in a non-stick frying pan.

* Have all your fillings prepared before starting to cook.

* Move the omelette around in the pan to create texture while it's cooking.

* For a proper French omelette don't cook it completely. Serve it while still a little runny, or 'baveuse' as the French say (the actual translation of this is dribble or drool. Much tastier than it sounds!).

POACHED EGGS

* For perfectly shaped poached eggs, use the freshest eggs you can find.

* Make sure the water is at a rolling boil before turning it down to a medium heat.

* Swirl the water but let it die down a little before you add the egg, otherwise there will be too much movement and the yolk will detach itself from the white.

* For ease, poach eggs one at a time – they're more likely to break if there's more than one in the pan.

* Use a slotted spoon to turn the egg halfway through the cooking time.

* Drain the poached eggs on kitchen paper before serving.

* If poaching more than one egg, cook them all separately, set aside, then heat them up together in boiling water for 20–30 seconds at the end of the cooking time.

BAKED EGGS, TARTS AND QUICHES

* You must bake eggs at a really low temperature otherwise they will soufflé: 140°C/gas 1 is perfect.

* If you don't have a fan oven, cook these dishes on the bottom shelf as it is cooler than the top.

* When baking egg custards, cook them in a bain-marie (a tin or other container of boiled water) so they cook gently. Always make sure the water in the bain-marie comes halfway up the sides of the ramekin or dish the eggs are being baked in.

* Egg-based dishes should be slightly under-cooked and still have some wobble, otherwise they will taste and look like scrambled eggs when you cut into them. And, remember, they will continue to firm up a little while cooling.

The Perfect FRIED EGG

Serves 1

2 tablespoons vegetable, corn or sunflower oil
1 large free-range egg

Heat the oil in a frying pan until fairly hot, but by no means smoking. Crack the egg into a small cup or ramekin (this makes it easier to avoid breakages in the pan), then add gently to the pan. The egg should begin to set immediately: if it starts to spit like crazy, turn down the heat. You want your egg to set at a reasonable pace, not too slowly, but not too fast. I like it when my egg is a bit crispy on the bottom – that way you know it has been fried rather than poached in the oil.

Once the white has almost set, tilt the pan to fill a tablespoon with the hot oil and baste the egg yolk. Keep basting until an opaque layer of egg white covers the top. Remove the egg from the pan with a fish slice and drain briefly on a piece of kitchen paper.

The Perfect BOILED EGG

Serves 1

2 large free-range eggs
sea salt

Bring a small pan of salted water to the boil. (Yes, I know salted water sounds strange, but eggshells are porous and the salt will season the egg.) Lower your eggs gently into the boiling water, making sure they are fully immersed, then leave them to boil for exactly 4 minutes – not a minute more, not a minute less for a perfectly runny egg. For an egg that is slightly set but not runny (such as for salads), boil for 5 minutes, and for a hard-boiled egg, boil for 7 minutes. Remove the egg from the water and you're ready to go.

If you're planning to eat the egg from an eggcup, make sure you place it rounded end facing up, as that is where the yolk sits in the egg.

If you want to eat the egg warm in a salad, peel it under cold, running water.

If you want to eat a hard-boiled egg cold, leave it to cool for 30 minutes in iced water (this will also avoid dark rings round the yolk).

WHY NOT TRY?

Marmite soldiers: Serve your soft-boiled egg with soft or toasted soldiers spread with loads of butter and a fine layer of Marmite.

Soft-boiled eggs with truffle and asparagus: Peel and mash your soft-boiled eggs, then mix them with a fine grating of fresh truffle (if you can't get your hands on fresh, use jarred) and some salt and pepper. Serve with steamed asparagus stalks and a little melted butter.

Quails' eggs: Use the same technique when boiling quails' eggs. As you are more likely to boil quite a few at once, the cooking time is the same.

Perfect SCRAMBLED EGGS

Serves 1

1 tablespoon butter
2 large free-range eggs
1 tablespoon milk
sea salt and freshly ground black pepper

Heat a small frying pan over a low to medium heat and add the butter. In a small mixing bowl, lightly beat together the eggs, milk, salt and pepper. When the butter starts to foam, swirl it around the pan and pour in the eggs.

With a wooden spoon, start to scrape away at the bottom of the pan and lift up the folds of setting egg. Keep doing this until the pan has lots of 'feathers' of egg, but there is still about 20 per cent liquid – you're looking for a slightly loose, creamy texture. Give the eggs a quick stir and they're ready to serve.

WHY NOT TRY?

Smoked salmon and scrambled eggs: Halve and toast a white bagel and spread with butter. Lay a couple of slices of smoked salmon on each bagel half, and top with scrambled eggs.

Mexican scrambled eggs: For a delicious quick supper, fry 4 slices of cured chorizo until crisp and set aside. Pour the chorizo cooking oil into a small pan. Add 2 chopped spring onions, 1 sliced red chilli and ½ sliced green pepper and fry for 2 minutes. Add 2 beaten eggs to the pan and stir until scrambled. Pour the eggs on to a toasted flour tortilla and serve with the crisp chorizo slices and plenty of chopped coriander.

The Perfect POACHED EGG

Serves 1

1 large free-range egg
½ teaspoon salt
1 teaspoon white wine vinegar

Crack the egg into a ramekin or small cup (this gives you more control over the egg; trying to crack an egg straight into the water almost always ends in disaster). Bring a medium-sized pan of water to the boil. Add the salt and vinegar (the vinegar will fizz up, which always adds a touch of excitement to the occasion!).

When the pan has reached a rolling boil, turn it down to a medium heat. Give the water a good stir, then allow it to settle for a couple of seconds before plonking your egg into the centre of the whirling water. What you want to see is the egg forming a teardrop shape while the water is still swirling round it; if the water is swirling too much, though, the egg may start to break up, and if the water is not swirling enough, it will lack any shape.

Leave the egg to poach for 2 minutes before removing it from the water with a slotted spoon. While it's poaching there needs to be the odd bubble rising to the surface of the water, but it should certainly not reach a rolling boil. The egg will float to the surface when it's ready. Remove it with a slotted spoon and allow to dry for a few seconds on kitchen paper.

Smoked haddock & CREVETTE
FISHCAKES WITH A POACHED EGG

I know peeling crevettes can be a bit of a faff, but the flavour and meatiness you get from them is well worth the hassle. Paired with smoked fish and a soft poached egg, this has to be one of the most comforting meals anyone could ask for. If you're feeling really extravagant, why not have it with hollandaise sauce (see page 242)?

To make the fishcakes, put the potatoes into a small pan, cover with cold water and add a pinch of salt. Bring the water to the boil and cook the potatoes for 10–15 minutes, or until soft, then drain. Pop the potatoes back into the pan and mash them, but do not add any butter or milk. Transfer the mashed potatoes to a bowl and leave to cool.

Lay the haddock – skin side up – in a frying pan and cover with cold water. Bring to the boil for 1 minute, then switch the heat off. Leave the fish to cool for 10 minutes in the pan of water. This will produce a perfectly poached piece of fish. Remove the fish from the water and leave it to drain on kitchen paper.

Preheat the oven to 180ºC/gas 4. When the haddock has cooled enough to touch, peel off the skin and break the flesh up into large flakes. Add the flaked fish to the potatoes, then add the whole peeled prawns, mixed herbs, lemon zest and seasoning. Roll your sleeves up and get your hands in there! Shape into 4 even-sized balls and flatten them.

Put the flour, beaten egg and breadcrumbs on three separate plates. Dip the fishcakes first into the flour, then into the beaten egg, then into the breadcrumbs.

Whack a frying pan on the hob and heat a good lug of olive oil until the oil sizzles when you pop a few breadcrumbs in. Lay the fishcakes in the pan and fry over a medium heat for 3–4 minutes on each side, making sure they're golden all over. Remove the fishcakes from the pan and drain on kitchen paper. Keep them warm in the oven while you poach the eggs.

Bring a medium-sized pan of water to the boil and poach your eggs, one at a time. Reheat them together just before serving (see page 41). Serve the fishcakes on a bed of spinach, topped with a poached egg.

Serves 4
Preparation time 40 minutes
Cooking time 15 minutes

4 free-range eggs
steamed spinach, to serve

For the fishcakes
200g potatoes (e.g. a large baking potato), peeled and cubed
400g undyed smoked haddock fillet
20 crevettes (cooked, shell-on prawns), shelled, or 200g small shelled cooked prawns
2 tablespoons chopped mixed herbs, such as chervil, dill and parsley
zest of 1 unwaxed lemon
sea salt and freshly ground black pepper
100g plain flour
1 free-range egg, lightly beaten
200g breadcrumbs
olive oil

Smoked salmon,
GOAT'S CHEESE & PEA TART

The smokiness of the salmon, mixed with the creaminess of the goat's cheese and the freshness of the peas, brings a multidimensional extravaganza of flavours to this tart and makes it as fantastic for a family summer lunch as it is for a starter at a formal dinner party.

Preheat the oven to 170°C/gas 3. Heat the olive oil in a small frying pan. Add the red onion and fry on a fairly high heat for 5 minutes, or until slightly charred but beginning to soften. Remove from the pan and set aside.

Pour the white wine into a pan and boil on a high heat for 5 minutes, or until the wine has reduced by two-thirds and is syrupy. Pour into a mixing bowl and leave to cool for 5 minutes.

Neatly scatter the red onions, smoked salmon strips, peas and goat's cheese into the pastry tart case. Add the eggs, cream and Parmesan to the mixing bowl containing the reduced white wine and whisk together. Season well with salt and pepper and stir in the herbs. Pour into a measuring jug.

Place the tart case on a baking tray and pour in the liquid – the mixture will come fairly high up the edge of the tart case. Place carefully on the bottom shelf of the oven, as the lower heat will stop the tart cooking too fast and prevent it rising like a soufflé. Bake for 30 minutes, or until the tart begins to turn golden. You want it to still have a little wobble but it should not be runny at all. Remove from the oven and leave to cool on a wire rack. Serve warm or cold.

Serves 6
Preparation time 30 minutes
Cooking time 1 hour

2 teaspoons olive oil
1 small red onion, peeled and cut into small wedges
100ml white wine
120g smoked salmon, cut into thin strips
120g fresh peas
100g soft goat's cheese
1 portion foolproof shortcrust pastry (see page 211), baked blind in a 17cm tart tin (see page 210)
3 free-range eggs
150ml double cream
30g Parmesan cheese, grated
sea salt and freshly ground black pepper
1 tablespoon chopped mixed fresh herbs, such as dill, mint and chives

WHY NOT TRY?

Courgette, red onion, feta and mint: Using a potato peeler, slice 2 courgettes lengthways into ribbons. Pile them up in the tart case and scatter over 100g of feta cheese, 1 small red onion, cut into wedges then sautéd as above, and 1 tablespoon of chopped fresh mint.

CHEAT

If you really don't have the time or inclination to make pastry, there are some amazingly good all-butter pastry cases on the market today. Look out for organic ones, as they tend to have fewer additives.

Rosewater & CARDAMOM CRÈME BRÛLÉE WITH pistachios

You'll see that North African influences are strong in these aromatic little puds. The cardamom and rosewater complement the creamy custard, and the pistachio transforms this familiar dish.

Serves 4
Preparation time 15 minutes
Cooking time 30 minutes
Cooling time 2½ hours

570ml double cream
5 cardamom pods
6 free-range egg yolks
7 tablespoons golden caster sugar
2 tablespoons rosewater
1 teaspoon vanilla extract
2 tablespoons pistachio nuts, chopped

In a small pan, heat the cream and cardamom really slowly until tiny bubbles start to show around the edges, so that the cardamom infuses the cream with flavour. Meanwhile, mix the egg yolks with 3 tablespoons of sugar in a bowl. Remove the cardamon pods from the pan and then with a balloon whisk, whisk in the hot double cream really quickly until it has all combined. Add the rosewater and vanilla extract and leave to infuse for 10 minutes.

Preheat the oven to 140°C/gas 1. Divide the infused custard between 4 ramekins. Lay a piece of kitchen paper in the bottom of a roasting tray and place the ramekins in the roasting tray. Boil the kettle and add enough boiling water to come halfway up the sides of the ramekins in the roasting tray. Place the tray on the lowest shelf of the oven and bake for 30 minutes, checking 5 minutes before they are due to be finished – you want them to be like a wobbly, loose jelly, as they will set more as they cool. If you cook them until they are fully set they will taste eggy and may even scramble a bit.

Remove the roasting tray from the oven and take the ramekins out. Leave to cool at room temperature for 30 minutes, then place in the fridge for at least 2 hours or overnight.

When you're ready to serve the crème brûlées, dust the tops with the remaining 4 tablespoons of sugar. Using a cook's blowtorch or under a very hot grill, heat until the sugar has turned golden and caramelised. Give the topping a minute or two to set (this may take a little longer if done under the grill), then sprinkle with pistachios to serve.

Dead posh CHEESE & TRUFFLE SOUFFLÉ FOR TWO

This may sound like some mega-gastro experience, but truffle cheeses are readily available these days and are an inexpensive way to get some truffle action! Give it a go – I promise you'll find soufflé-making much less intimidating than it's made out to be.

Serves 2
Preparation time 10 minutes
Cooking time 25 minutes

15g butter, plus extra for greasing the dish
30g Parmesan cheese, plus extra for dusting
1 tablespoon plain flour
150ml milk
55g truffle Pecorino cheese
3 free-range eggs, separated
1 teaspoon truffle oil (optional)
sea salt and freshly ground black pepper

WHY NOT TRY?

If you can't find truffle cheese, or just want a regular cheese soufflé, replace it with Cheddar or Gruyère and don't bother with the truffle oil.

Preheat the oven to 200°C/gas 6. Grease a medium-sized ramekin (big enough for 2 servings) with butter, then grate a fine layer of Parmesan over it to coat the inside of the dish.

Melt the 15g of butter in a small pan, stir in the flour and cook over a low heat for 1 minute. Remove from the heat and gradually add the milk bit by bit, whisking as you go to avoid any lumps forming. When the milk has been combined, return to the heat and keep stirring while it simmers lightly. Use a wooden spoon and scrape the bottom of the pan – milk burns easily and there is nothing more disgusting than white sauce that tastes of burnt milk.

After about 2 minutes, when the sauce has thickened, remove the pan from the heat. Stir in the truffle cheese, then the Parmesan, egg yolks and truffle oil (if using) and season well. Leave the mixture to cool for 10 minutes. In a clean, dry mixing bowl, whisk the egg whites until they are stiff, but not too solid.

Mix a spoonful of egg white into the cheese sauce, to loosen it. Now pour the cheese mixture into the rest of the egg white and, using a metal spoon, fold them together as quickly and lightly as possible – try not to knock the air out of the soufflé mixture as this will affect the rise and texture of the dish.

Pour the mixture into the ramekin and level off the top. Push the tip of a knife 8mm into the edge of the ramekin and slide it right round, as if you're pulling the soufflé mixture away from the edge – this is what will make it rise. Put the soufflé on a baking sheet and place in the oven to cook for 18 minutes, until it's risen, firm but not too stiff – it should still be gooey in the middle. Remove from the oven and serve straight away. It will sink a little bit after a few minutes, so the sooner you serve it, the better the 'wow' factor!

4
PASTA & RISOTTO

Can you conceive of a world without pasta? I have no idea what my diet would be made up of in such a place, as I cook pasta all the time. It's one of the easiest, tastiest and most nutritious things we can eat – a power food, they say. Served with the right sauce, it becomes a well-balanced meal, with carbohydrates, protein from meat or fish and fibre and vitamins from veggies. It can also be quick to prepare, which is partly why we eat so much of it in this country.

Most of us start by learning to cook a basic tomato or bolognese sauce. And there are many techniques used in making pasta sauces: chopping veg; sweating them; browning meat; slow cooking. Then there's knowing how to cook pasta, which for the record should be a little undercooked – 'al dente' – so it keeps its bite.

While some pasta sauces are speedy to prepare such as my version of a carbonara with smoked salmon, sometimes it's nice to indulge in a bit of long, slow cooking, like when making a proper ragù, where you get to torture your taste buds while the smell of your creation wafts through the house. But this is the pleasure of cooking, so remember the saying: the best things come to those who wait.

With risotto, slow cooking is also the name of the game. What you have to remember too is to use good rice, good wine, good stock, great additions and really put your heart into the cooking. Making fantastic risotto is a slow process. You need a lot of patience and strong arm muscles, but believe me, it's always worth it.

✩ ★ Pasta Tips & Tricks ★ ✩

I know we have some super fresh pasta available to us nowadays, but why not, once you're feeling confident with the sauces, give pasta-making a go? It's surprisingly easy and good fun to use a bit of elbow grease and run around the kitchen with lengths of fresh pasta.

COOKING PASTA

* Invest in a good pasta fork or tongs, as it makes everything so much easier, especially when you're trying to take cooked, slippery pasta out of boiling water!

* Boil pasta in the biggest pot you have and add a teaspoon of salt to the water.

* Make sure you plunge pasta into water that is boiling so much it is rolling rather than bubbling.

* Pasta should be eaten *al dente*, which means 'to the bite'. I would generally suggest tasting it a minute before its cooking time is up to check whether or not it's cooked. Also remember that fresh pasta cooks much more quickly than dried.

* Always leave about 3 tablespoons of the water the pasta has boiled in at the bottom of the pan, as this makes the sauce silky and thickens it a bit at the end of cooking.

MATCHING SAUCES TO PASTAS

* Shaped pastas such as conchiglie, farfalle and fusilli pair well with all kinds of sauces, but especially those with texture. Pieces of meat, vegetable or bean are captured in the crevices of the pasta and nestle in the twists.

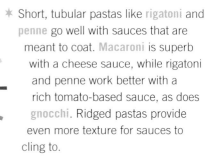

* Short, tubular pastas like rigatoni and penne go well with sauces that are meant to coat. Macaroni is superb with a cheese sauce, while rigatoni and penne work better with a rich tomato-based sauce, as does gnocchi. Ridged pastas provide even more texture for sauces to cling to.

* Long, thin dried pasta, such as capellini, spaghetti and linguine, marry best with olive-oil-based sauces. These long expanses of pasta need lots of lubrication.

* A lot of the recipes in this chapter make quite big vats of sauce. But don't worry about not being able to use it up in one go – pasta sauce freezes brilliantly!

Making Pasta FROM SCRATCH

Makes about 1kg
Preparation time 30 minutes
Resting time 30 minutes

600g '00' Italian pasta flour
6 large free-range eggs (or, for a richer pasta,
12 egg yolks)

Pop the flour into your food processor and give it a quick whiz. This will do the same thing as sifting it. Turn the processor on full, then tip the eggs in through the funnel. It will quickly resemble breadcrumbs. Turn the pasta out on to the kitchen surface and start to knead: this is really important, as kneading will allow the gluten to develop the way it does with bread dough. This in turn creates the pasta's firm and 'bitey' texture, which is what you're looking for. If you don't knead it properly, your dough will be too soft and can break when you roll it out.

To knead pasta dough, pull it backwards and forwards along the work surface. Squash it, pull it and stretch it in all directions – it's hard work wrestling with dough, but it's a good way to get all your aggression out! The pasta will start to become springy and silky within a few minutes. Wrap the pasta dough tightly in clingfilm, so it doesn't dry out, and leave it to rest in the fridge for 30 minutes.

There are two techniques to rolling out your dough:

★ **Rolling method:** Cut the pasta dough into 4 pieces. Take one piece (making sure you keep the rest of the dough airtight in the clingfilm), and roll it into a ball. Dust the work surface and rolling pin lightly with '00' flour or semolina flour. Roll each piece of dough out as thinly as you can. Repeat with the rest of the pasta dough. You will end up with giant pasta circles, rather than long strips. Don't fret: cutting the dough into pasta shapes uses the same method (see below), whether you make it by hand or in a machine.

★ **Machine method:** To begin with, clamp your pasta machine firmly to a clean work surface. Make sure you have enough room to work: once you start making the pasta you will be surprised how long the pieces get and you may find it takes over the whole of your kitchen. Start by cutting your pasta dough into 4 pieces. Take one piece (making sure you keep the rest of the dough airtight in the clingfilm), then squash it out flat with your fingers. Set the pasta machine at the widest setting. Dust the pasta machine with '00' flour. Tease the pasta dough through the machine while you turn the handle. If you find your pasta is sticking, dust it with some more flour.

Take the machine down to the next setting and roll the pasta through again. Fold the pasta in half, and put it through the machine for the third time, with the straight edges going through at the sides. Take the setting down again and repeat. Keep going, reducing the setting every other time you roll out the dough. As you move down the settings, you will see that the pasta is becoming thinner and longer, and what you are looking for is a lovely silky piece of dough with straight edges. Get to the second thinnest setting if you're making sheet pasta like lasagne or tagliatelle, and to the thinnest setting for filled pasta like ravioli or tortellini.

Once your pasta is thin enough, shape or cut it straight away because it will dry out really quickly.

SHAPING PASTA

* **Lasagne:** To make lasagne sheets, cut the pasta into large rectangular sheets. If you are trying to replicate commercial bought lasagne, each sheet needs to be about 25 x 15cm, but as lasagne is a sheet pasta you can cut it to fit whatever dish you're using.

* **Pappardelle:** Neaten the edges of the rolled-out dough, dust it lightly with flour, and roll it up. Cut it into 2.5cm-thick slices. When you unravel them, they will look like thick ribbons.

* **Tagliatelle:** Cut the pasta dough out as for pappardelle, but only into 8mm-thick ribbons as tagliatelle is narrower.

* **Ravioli:** With a round 5cm or 6cm pastry cutter, cut out lots of circles. Using half the circles, place a teaspoon of the filling of your choice in the centre, then with a wet pastry brush wipe the edges and stick the rest of the pasta circles on top, pressing the air out as you go. Seal the edges by cutting out with a slightly smaller pastry cutter.

* **Tortellini:** Start off in the same way as making ravioli, but this time you don't need to keep half the circles free. With a damp pastry brush, wet the outside edge of the pasta, then fold the pasta in half so the edges touch and it becomes a filled semi-circle. Press the air out and press down the edges. Place your finger in the middle, then twist each of the pointed edges into each other to make it like a navel shape.

Gnocchi
Serves 6–8

I recently discovered that the word gnocchi actually means 'lumps', which made me chuckle as there is no better word to describe these little pillows of potato pasta. The great thing about gnocchi is that it's a terrific change from regular pasta and really easy to cook too.

Preparation time 35 minutes
Cooking time 2 minutes

500g medium floury potatoes
1 large free-range egg, beaten
sea salt and freshly ground black pepper
250g flour ('00' if you can find it, but it's not crucial for gnocchi), plus extra for dusting

Boil the unpeeled potatoes in a large pan of water for 25 minutes or until tender. Drain, and, when cool enough to handle, remove the skins. Mash the potatoes until really smooth. Add the egg, plenty of salt and pepper and the flour and mix to a dough. Turn out and knead on a floured work surface for a few minutes.

Cut the dough into 4 pieces, roll out each piece into 2cm-thick 'ropes' (basically long thick strings of dough) then cut each rope into 2.5cm pieces. Squeeze the gnocchi gently in the middle to make them look like little pillows. Leave to dry out for 10 minutes on a floured work surface. Next, and in batches, place the gnocchi pillows in a large pan of boiling salted water for 2 minutes, or until they rise to the surface.

If you aren't using them straightaway, you can leave them out to dry for up to 2 hours. They will also keep in the fridge for 2 days.

WHY NOT TRY?

GNOCCHI WITH TOMATO AND MOZZARELLA SAUCE
Make a batch of fresh tomato sauce (see page 240), and stir in a ball of buffalo mozzarella and a handful of torn basil for the last 5 minutes of cooking. Stir through the cooked gnocchi to serve.

COOKING RISOTTO ☆

* Use the best risotto rice you can find. I really like carnaroli, but look out for arborio and vialone nano, which are also fantastic. You do need proper risotto rice though; don't attempt it with any other kind.

* Make sure the onions are really softened, but don't have too much colour. You need them to be sweet, as this is where a lot of a risotto's flavour comes from. Risotto with under cooked onions is not enjoyable to eat!

* Use the best quality stock, as most of a risotto's flavour will be determined by this – homemade is best, but the fresh stuff from the supermarkets is great too.

RISOTTO

* Ensure that the stock is hot before you start to cook your risotto.

* Cook risotto over a medium heat – too high and the stock will evaporate; too low and the risotto will take ages and risk over cooking.

* Keep stirring the risotto to release the starch from the rice grains, as this will give a creamy texture.

* Stir cold butter through at the end to make the risotto extra creamy.

* Grate your Parmesan really finely so that it melts quickly.

WHY NOT TRY?

RISOTTO ARANCINI BALLS

A dazzling way to use up any leftover risotto is to make arancini. When the risotto is fridge-cold, scoop out a teaspoonful and flatten it in the palm of your hand. Push a 1cm cube of mozzarella into the centre and shape the risotto round it like a ball. Coat the ball in flour, then egg, then breadcrumbs, and fry until crisp and golden. Serve with salad as a light lunch, starter or snack

Aubergine, artichoke
& LAMB BOLOGNESE

To get the best out of this recipe you need to cook the aubergine to the point where it has lost a lot of its water and is quite caramelised, as this will encourage a sweet, sticky sauce. Trofie or strozzapreti offer more to get your teeth into than more familiar pasta shapes, and the edges become a little rough after cooking so that sauce clings to each piece. This pasta does take slightly longer than regular pasta to cook, but make sure you cook it only until al dente!

Serves 4–6
Preparation time 10 minutes
Cooking time 1½ hours

50ml olive oil
2 medium aubergines, chopped into 1cm cubes
sea salt and freshly ground black pepper
500g minced lamb
1 onion, peeled and finely chopped
4 garlic cloves, peeled and finely chopped
300ml white wine
300ml lamb or chicken stock
a small pinch of saffron
1 x 400g tin of chopped tomatoes
2 tablespoons tomato purée
a small bunch of fresh parsley, chopped
a few sprigs of fresh thyme, chopped
½ tin or jar of artichokes (about 4–5 artichokes), drained, then cut into small chunks
350–550g fresh trofie or strozzapreti pasta (depending on whether you're serving 4 or 6 people)
freshly torn basil and Pecorino cheese, to serve

Heat the oil in a large, heavy-based pan. Sprinkle the aubergines with a little salt, then fry for 15 minutes over a medium high heat until softened and browned (it is best to do this in batches). Remove the aubergines with a slotted spoon so you leave some oil in the pan, and drain them on kitchen paper.

Add the minced lamb to the pan and season with a little salt. Brown the lamb, then transfer to a bowl with a slotted spoon. Finally, fry the onion in the oil left in the pan for 5–8 minutes or until the onion is softened and slightly golden, adding the garlic for the last minute of cooking time.

Return the lamb to the pan and add the white wine, stock, saffron (don't use too much as it can be overpowering), chopped tomatoes, tomato purée, parsley and thyme. Give it all a good mix and, when it starts to bubble, add the fried aubergines and the artichokes. Leave to bubble away on a low heat for an hour with the lid slightly askew until the sauce is reduced by a third.

Ten minutes before you're ready to serve, cook the pasta in lots of boiling, salted water according to the instructions on the packet (checking it in its last minutes of cooking as you need it still to have some bite!). Drain the pasta and stir through enough sauce to coat. Divide between pasta bowls to serve, and sprinkle with basil and Pecorino.

WHY NOT TRY?

Make a gnocchi bolognese bake.Mix the bolognese with some parboiled gnocchi (see page 56). Top with béchamel sauce (see page 238) and mozzarella cheese, then bake in the oven for 30 minutes.

Proper MEAT RAGÙ

Much as everyone loves a good 'ole 'spag bol', going that extra length and making a proper ragù makes all the difference. A true ragù uses stewing cuts that are shredded through the sauce when meltingly soft. I have put veal and pork in my sauce, but you can play around with whichever meats you like. Veal adds a richness and stickiness that you don't get with any other meat. Use British rose veal if you can; it is ethically reared. I have suggested you serve the ragù with fresh pappardelle, but this sauce is just as happy with penne as it is cosying up to some creamy polenta. It also makes a mean lasagne.

Serves 4–6
Preparation time 20 minutes
Cooking time 2½ hours

2 tablespoons olive oil

400g veal or beef shin, chopped into 4cm chunks

400g pork leg, chopped into 4cm chunks

2 medium onions, peeled and chopped

2 carrots, peeled and chopped

2 celery stalks, chopped

4 garlic cloves, peeled and chopped

2 tablespoons tomato purée

2 bay leaves

a few sprigs of fresh thyme, chopped

1 sprig of fresh rosemary, finely chopped

a few sprigs of fresh parsley, chopped

400ml red or white wine

400ml beef or veal stock

1 x 400g tin of chopped tomatoes

a small bunch of fresh basil, torn

300–450g pappardelle, preferably fresh (see page 55–6)

lots of freshly grated Parmesan cheese, to serve

Preheat the oven to 170°C/gas 2. Heat the olive oil in a large casserole, add the meat in batches, and cook until it is nicely golden brown all over. Remove to a bowl with a slotted spoon and set aside. Throw the onions, carrots and celery into the pan and cook on a fairly low heat for 15 minutes, or until the vegetables have softened and gone slightly golden. For the last 2 minutes of cooking add the garlic.

Stir in the tomato purée and cook for another minute. Add the bay leaves, thyme, rosemary, parsley, wine, stock, tomatoes and half the basil. Return the meat and all its lovely juices to the pan. Give everything a good stir, then put the lid on and place in the oven for 2 hours. You want the meat to be really soft and the sauce to thicken and become rich.

Remove the casserole from the oven and leave to rest for 10 minutes, then go to it with two forks and shred the meat to bits. If the meat is cooked properly, it will break up as you squish it a little with the back of a wooden spoon.

Meanwhile, bring a large pan of salted water to the boil and cook the pappardelle for 2–3 minutes. Drain, then return the pasta to the pan and stir in enough sauce to generously coat it. Serve with the rest of the basil and loads of grated Parmesan.

Fried gnocchi WITH TOMATO & GOAT'S CHEESE sauce

As scrummy as gnocchi are in their own right, frying them gently in butter lifts them to a whole new level: the middles are like fluffy clouds of potato and the outsides become crispy and golden like a potato croquette. I have a great friend who swears by them for breakfast with bacon and eggs. Here, I have teamed the gnocchi with a sweet tomato sauce infused with creamy goat's cheese, as they complement each other brilliantly, but the sauce would make a fantastic accompaniment to penne or ravioli too.

Heat the oil in a saucepan. Add the onion and fry slowly for 8 minutes or until it has softened and begun to turn golden. Add the garlic and fry for a further minute. Tip in the chopped tomatoes, tomato paste or purée, sherry vinegar, Tabasco, sugar, half the basil and salt and pepper and leave to bubble away gently on a low heat for 20 minutes. The sauce will have thickened up nicely by this stage.

Crumble in the goat's cheese and stir gently as if to tease it into melting.

Heat the butter in a frying pan and add the precooked gnocchi (in batches). Fry them for 2 minutes on each side, or until they have crisped up and are golden. Drain the gnocchi on kitchen paper and serve with a dollop of sauce, the remaining torn basil and a grating of Parmesan.

Serves 4
Preparation time 15 minutes
Cooking time 20 minutes

1 batch of freshly made gnocchi (see page 56), or 500g fresh shop-bought gnocchi, cooked for 2 minutes in salted, boiling water
30g butter
Parmesan cheese, to serve

For the sauce
1 tablespoon olive oil
1 onion, peeled and finely chopped
3 garlic cloves, peeled and finely chopped
1 x 400g tin of chopped tomatoes
1 tablespoon sun-dried tomato paste or tomato purée
a splash of good-quality sherry vinegar
a few splashes of Tabasco
1 teaspoon sugar
a small bunch of fresh basil, torn
sea salt and freshly ground black pepper
100g fresh soft goat's cheese

Creamy smoked salmon
& PEA SPAGHETTI

Spaghetti carbonara is a classic for a reason, but it is laden with cream and, therefore, also very guilt-inducing. So I decided to halve the cream content and replace the rest with Greek yoghurt. Having done this, it seemed natural to replace the smokiness of the bacon with smoked salmon. I then decided to add some green colour with the summery addition of broad beans and green peas, my favourite veggies, and finished with a hint of lemon to lift the dish.

Serves 4
Preparation time 15 minutes
Cooking time 10 minutes

350g dried spaghetti
150g podded and shelled broad beans
150g fresh or frozen garden peas
200ml double cream
200ml Greek yoghurt
2 large free-range egg yolks
35g Parmesan cheese
zest of 1 unwaxed lemon
sea salt and freshly ground black pepper
180g smoked salmon (about 8 slices), sliced
    into short ribbons
a small bunch of fresh chives, snipped

Bring a large pan of salted water to the boil and cook the spaghetti according to the instructions on the packet. For the last 3 minutes of the cooking time add the broad beans and peas.

Meanwhile mix together the cream, yoghurt, egg yolks, Parmesan, lemon zest, salt and pepper.

Drain the cooked pasta, beans and peas, leaving a few tablespoons of water in the bottom of the pan. Return the pan to a low heat and pour in the sauce. Toss the pasta in the sauce, then add the smoked salmon and chives, giving it all a good mix round until it's evenly incorporated and the salmon has cooked through. Serve piping hot.

WHY NOT TRY? If you like things quite lemony, add the zest of the whole lemon; otherwise, use just half.

Open LASAGNE WITH CRAB & *prawns in pink sauce*

I know this recipe may sound quite strange as you end up boiling prawn shells, but what you're actually doing is making a really rich and luxurious prawn stock that's along the lines of a bisque. Once it has reduced and you've added the cream, it becomes an elegant, velvety sauce, which goes so naturally with plump prawns and sweet white crabmeat. Open lasagne is a novel and, in this case stylish, way of eating pasta, as you find sumptuous ingredients hiding under the sheets.

Serves 4
Preparation time 20 minutes
Cooking time 50 minutes

3 tablespoons olive oil
1 onion, peeled and chopped
2 carrots, chopped
2 celery stalks, chopped
3 garlic cloves, peeled but left whole
2 bay leaves
a few sprigs of fresh thyme, leaves picked
a few fresh parsley stalks
1 tablespoon tomato purée
24 raw king prawns, peeled, shells reserved
a good lug of brandy
1.5 litres fish stock
200g freshly picked white crabmeat
a squeeze of lemon juice
200ml double cream
8 sheets fresh lasagne (from the fridge section of the supermarket), cut in half width-ways
1 vine-ripened tomato, seeded and chopped
fresh chervil, to garnish

Heat 2 tablespoons of olive oil in a large heavy-bottomed saucepan. Toss in the onions, carrots, celery, garlic and herbs and sauté really slowly for about 20 minutes. This process is very important, as it is how you will get most of the flavour; what you want is for the vegetables to sweat really slowly and get incredibly soft before they start to caramelise a little. You want some colour, but not too much.

Stir in the tomato purée and coat all the vegetables. You need to cook the purée for 1 minute to get rid of its raw flavour. Whack the heat up and add the prawn shells, but no prawn meat at this stage. Sauté the shells until they have gone bright pink, then douse with the brandy and add the stock, which should cover the shells. Cook for 20 minutes on a slow boil.

Pour the sauce through a sieve, squashing the shells so they release all their juices. Transfer the strained stock to a frying pan and boil it gently to reduce the sauce by half.

Add the prawns, crabmeat and a squeeze of lemon juice to the sauce and poach for 2 minutes, or until the prawns are nicely opaque and cooked through. Stir in the cream and take the sauce off the heat while you prepare your pasta.

Bring a pan of salted water to the boil and add a lug of olive oil. Drop in the lasagne sheets one by one. Doing this and using the oil will stop them sticking. When cooked, drain the lasagne and lay a sheet on each plate. Top each sheet with a few prawns, some crabmeat and a drizzle of sauce. Repeat and then top with a couple of prawns, and scatter with chopped tomato and chervil to serve.

Pancetta, borlotti bean & RADICCHIO risotto

Here I've combined smoky pancetta, creamy borlotti beans and bitter radicchio to make a soothing risotto that's a great week-night supper as well as impressive enough for a dinner party.

Heat the oil and butter in a heavy-bottomed pan. Fry the onion and pancetta over a lowish heat for 10 minutes, or until the pancetta has turned golden and the onions have softened. For the last minute of cooking, add the garlic and thyme to the pan.

Add the rice and stir for a minute or two to coat the grains of rice. Pour over the wine and keep stirring while it is absorbed. Gradually ladle the hot stock into the risotto, letting it be absorbed between each ladleful. Keep stirring it, as this encourages the starch to come out, which is what gives risotto its creamy texture.

With your last ladleful of stock add the beans and radicchio. The rice is ready when the grains are cooked but still have a little bite and the rice is loose but not soupy. Add in the butter and Parmesan, which will make the risotto rich and velvety. Serve with a scattering of basil leaves and, for those of you feeling extra wicked, why not have some more Parmesan?

Serves 4
Preparation time 15 minutes
Cooking time 30 minutes

1 tablespoon olive oil
1 tablespoon butter
1 onion, peeled and finely chopped
280g cubetti di pancetta
3 garlic cloves, peeled and finely chopped
a few sprigs of fresh thyme, leaves picked
250g risotto rice
1 glass of white wine
500ml hot chicken or vegetable stock
400g cooked borlotti beans (if you can cook your own you will see such a difference, but drained tinned ones are fine)
1 small head of radicchio, finely sliced
30g butter
30g grated Parmesan cheese
a handful of fresh basil leaves, torn

WHY NOT TRY?

Butternut squash risotto: Swap the borlotti beans and radicchio for ½ a butternut squash that has been cubed, then roasted in olive oil in the oven at 200°C/gas 6 for 25 minutes, then blended to a purée. Mix this purée through the risotto at the end of the cooking time and add a little bit more Parmesan. Delicious dressed with rocket leaves and a drizzle of olive oil.

Baked seafood
& SAFFRON RISOTTO

I was dubious when someone told me you could bake a risotto, thinking it wouldn't have its usual creaminess or become overcooked and lose its bite, but on experimenting I discovered otherwise, which is great for those days when you don't have the energy for all that stirring! This risotto makes a perfect dinner-party dish, and because you don't need to stand over it all the time, you also get to spend time with your guests.

Preheat the oven to 180°C/gas 4. Warm 2 tablespoons of olive oil in a large casserole dish and bung in the onions and chorizo. Sauté over a lowish heat for about 8 minutes, or until the onion has softened and turned slightly golden and the chorizo has released all its oil and coloured slightly . Add the garlic and fry for a further minute.

Stir in the rice and fry for a minute, then pour over the wine and stock and sprinkle in the saffron and paprika. Pop a lid on the casserole and place in the oven for 25 minutes.

Remove the casserole from the oven – the rice should by now have absorbed most of the liquid but will still be a little soupy. Increase the oven temperature to 200°C/gas 6. In a bowl, toss the prawns, shellfish, squid and monkfish in the remaining tablespoon of olive oil, then give the risotto a good stir and place the seafood on top. Pop the casserole back into the oven without the lid, and bake for a further 8 minutes. Remove from the oven and sprinkle with parsley. Give it one final stir and it's ready to serve.

Serves 4
Preparation time 20 minutes
Cooking time 50 minutes

3 tablespoons olive oil
1 onion, peeled and finely chopped
1 x 80g whole semi-dried or fresh chorizo
   sausage, chopped
3 garlic cloves, peeled and chopped
250g risotto rice
250ml white wine
600ml fish, chicken or vegetable stock
a pinch of saffron
a large pinch of smoked paprika
8 raw king prawns, peeled
8 mussels or clams (see page 107)
1 medium squid, cleaned and cut into pieces
   (with or without tentacles – see page 107)
150g monkfish, trimmed and cut into cubes
a small bunch of fresh, flat-leaf parsley,
   chopped

5

VEGETABLES

Despite the fact that there are many varieties of vegetables, when it comes to cooking with them, we still seem to do the same old, same old.

It's time to try something new. Take rainbow chard, for example, now that's a food that puts a spring in my step. The most beautiful vegetable out there, with the most intense flavour – what's not to love?

Then you have your root veggies, which tend to be either sweet as anything or, in the case of potatoes, real comfort food. Imagine a crappy day without chips, mash or roasties – even more crappy, methinks.

And think about how excited we get at the beginning of the year, knowing that spring is about to be sprung with its abundance of superb vegetables, from the first asparagus stalks in April through to pumpkins harvested at the beginning of winter. With so many vegetables to choose from throughout the year, it's no wonder that vegetable cookery can be so diverse.

★ TIPS & TRICKS ★

* Place root vegetables in cold, not boiling water, then bring to the boil and cook.

* When cooking green veggies, add them to boiling water.

* Plunge your veggies into iced water to cool them down quickly and retain their colour.

* Parboiling root vegetables and potatoes means that you cook them until they have started to cook on the outside and are a bit 'furry' or flaky, but are still firm and uncooked in the middle.

* Roasted vegetables need to go into piping hot oil to get maximum crispness.

VEG

* When steaming vegetables, don't keep removing the lid to check if the veggies are cooked, as this will make the steam disperse. Check them once you are pretty sure they are done.

* Don't over-boil the water when steaming vegetables – a slow simmer is just fine.

* Make sure when boiling vegetables there is enough water in the pan. Cover by at least 2.5cm of water.

* Aubergines and courgettes benefit from getting some colour on them, as they are pretty insipid without, especially when used in a stew or curry.

Sweating ONIONS (& CARROTS, CELERY & LEEKS)

Sweating an onion or a variety of vegetables at the beginning of cooking anything will determine how the whole dish tastes. The real aim of sweating onions and other vegetables is to slowly draw out the moisture, thus softening them and leaving the sugars neatly concentrated inside. I am going to explain to you how to do this with a basic onion, but the principle works with any 'mirepoix' vegetables, generally onions, carrots, celery or leeks. If you sweat your onions for only a matter of minutes, as most people do, you will not get the seriously rich flavour that's intended when casseroling your food.

1 tablespoon olive oil (or butter, or a spot of both)
1 or 2 onions, peeled and finely chopped

Over a highish heat, heat the oil or butter in a heavy-bottomed pan (size depending on what you're cooking). Once the oil is shimmering or the butter begins to foam, add the onions, stir and cover with a lid. Turn down the heat to its lowest setting and let the onions 'sweat' in the heat really gently. Every 2 minutes give them a quick stir to loosen them from the bottom of the pan. Be careful to watch for small pieces of onion scorching at the side of the pan. Cook the onions very slowly for about 10 minutes. They are ready when they are opaque and soft enough to squelch between your thumb and forefinger. If they keep their shape they need to cook a little longer. The onions should be lightly golden and taste sweet.

BLANCHING (& REFRESHING) VEGETABLES

To blanch or boil vegetables, bring a large pan of salted water to the boil. Once the water is at a rolling boil, add your vegetables to the pan. Boil them for 2–3 minutes, or until the vegetables are cooked through but retaining some 'bite'. Drain the veggies and either serve straight away or plunge them into iced water to stop them cooking, which also makes them keep their colour. You would 'refresh' your veg if you were going to cook them later on or par-cook them before adding them cold to a salad. You can blanch all vegetables except for root veg.

BOILING ROOT VEGETABLES

Place your root vegetables in a large pan of cold salted water and bring to the boil. Cook for around 15 minutes, or until cooked on the outside but still retaining some firmness in the middle.

PARBOILING

To parboil is to boil something in order to get it to a certain stage before cooking it further in another way, most commonly roasting. When parboiling your vegetables it is important to undercook them. You're looking for the vegetables to be cooked on the outside but uncooked in the middle.

STEAMING VEGETABLES

Steaming is without doubt the healthiest and tastiest way to cook vegetables. Not only does it retain more nutrients, it also keeps hold of more flavour. Steaming is easier than people think, and you don't need to have a load of swanky equipment to do it.

A sieve and a pan big enough to take the whole bowl part of the sieve will do. Simply pour a good 5cm of boiling water into the bottom of the pan, making sure you still have a good 5cm of space between the top of the water and the sieve. Place the sieve in the pan and your vegetables in the sieve. Bring the water to a constant simmer and pop a lid on the pan. The steam will cook the vegetables. For leafy green vegetables cook for 3–4 minutes; for firm green vegetables such as asparagus or beans cook for 4–5 minutes; and for new potatoes cook for about 18 minutes. While it takes a bit more time than boiling, don't underestimate the power of steam.

Perfect roast POTATOES

So simple – yet a crisp roast potato has to have been sent to us from food heaven. The secret is to heat the oil until it is piping hot, parboil the potatoes just enough so the outsides start to flake and the hot fat can make the edges extra crispy and to sprinkle them with sea salt before serving. In my opinion the only way to eat roast potatoes is to squash them with the back of your fork and drench them in gravy, but I'm sure we all have our own way!

Preheat the oven to 200°C/gas 6. Place the potatoes in a large pan, cover with cold water and add 1 teaspoon of salt. Bring to the boil, then cook for 7 minutes, until the potatoes are a bit 'furry' or flaky on the outside but still firm and uncooked in the middle. Drain them, giving them a bit of a shake in the colander or sieve so the edges become grainy – this will give you the crispiest potatoes.

Pour the oil into a large baking tray and pop it into the oven to heat for 5 minutes. Tip the drained, parboiled potatoes into the hot fat. Make sure each potato is coated in the oil, then roast in the oven for 1 hour, turning them every 20 minutes.

Remove the potatoes from the tray with a slotted spoon and drain on kitchen paper. Sprinkle generously with sea salt and serve.

Serves 4–6
Preparation time 10 minutes
Cooking time 1¼ hours

6 largish potatoes, peeled and quartered
sea salt
6 tablespoons olive oil, vegetable oil or, for a
    special occasion, goose fat

Creamy MASHED *potato*

Could mashed potato be the ultimate comfort food? On a cold winter's night, there's a lot to be said for tucking into a bowl of steamy mash drenched in butter. But mash can also be a pie topping and the base for many a dish. The secret to good mash is investing in a potato ricer (which looks like a giant garlic press), as opposed to the traditional potato masher. It will ensure you get lump-free restaurant-style 'pommes de terre purée'. Also, add the butter once the potato has been mashed and not while you're mashing it, or you will get lumps. The best mash is somewhere between fluffy and cloud-like, and smooth and creamy.

Serves 4
Preparation time 10 minutes
Cooking time 20 minutes

6 largish potatoes, peeled (I love Maris Pipers
   for mash)
sea salt and freshly ground black pepper
50g butter
50ml milk or cream

Place the potatoes in a large pan, cover with cold water and add 1 teaspoon of salt. Bring to the boil, and cook for 15 minutes or until softened and cooked through. Drain well and tip into a bowl.

Pop the potatoes, one at a time, into the potato ricer and squeeze them back into the pan: lots of squiggles of potato will spill out and there will be no lumps! (If you only have a classic potato masher, simply return the potatoes to the pan they were cooked in and mash like crazy until the potatoes are smooth.)

Place the pan on the hob over a medium heat and push the potato up the sides of the pan so you can see the base. Melt the butter and milk or cream in the centre of the base, then whip together with the fluffy potato until it holds its shape but isn't too stiff.

Season with plenty of salt and pepper and serve.

WHY NOT TRY?

Cheese mash: Add 85g of your favourite cheese – Cheddar, Stilton or goat's cheese – to the mash when you add the butter.

Mustard mash: Add 1–2 tablespoons of your favourite mustard to the mash when you add the butter.

Horseradish mash: Add 1–2 tablespoons horseradish to the mash when you add the butter.

Roasted garlic mash: Add a bulb or two of squeezed-out roasted garlic to the mash when you add the butter.

Colcannon: Add 6 chopped spring onions and 85g of shredded, cooked green cabbage to the mash when you add the butter.

Damn good DAUPHINOISE

Not exactly for the health-conscious, but every now and then a helping of dauphinoise goes down a treat, particularly with lamb. It can be made with crème fraîche, which actually makes it a fraction healthier and lighter, but some might argue that 'If you're gonna do it, do it properly!' If so, it has to be cream. You can use a mandolin to slice the potatoes really thinly, but watch your fingers!

Serves 4
Preparation time 15 minutes
Cooking time 40 minutes
Resting time 10 minutes

350ml milk
350ml double cream (or crème fraîche for a
    lighter and more authentic version)
1 large garlic clove, peeled and sliced
1 sprig of fresh thyme
1 bay leaf
sea salt and freshly ground black pepper
600g waxy potatoes (such as Maris Piper),
    peeled and really thinly sliced
30g Gruyère cheese, grated

Preheat the oven to 200°C/gas 6. Pour the milk and cream into a large pan, add the garlic, herbs and seasoning and bring to the boil. Turn down to a simmer for a couple of minutes.

Slide the potatoes into the pan and stir gently. Simmer for about 7 minutes, until the potato slices are only just tender; they should hold their shape and still have a good bite. Drain them in a colander over a bowl to catch the milk. Discard the thyme sprig and bay leaf.

Layer the potatoes in a shallow ovenproof dish, trickling some of the saved milk over each layer as you go. Pour more of the milk around the sides, but not too much – just enough so that when you press the potatoes down you can see it pool a little.

Sprinkle over the cheese, then place the dish in a shallow roasting tin (to catch the creamy dribbles) and bake for about 10–15 minutes, or until the cheese is beginning to bubble and turn golden brown. Allow to stand for 10 minutes before serving.

Roasted carrots
WITH ORANGE & *turmeric*

Slowly cooking carrots in butter is a classic method and as you're not boiling out all the flavour, the carrots with be seriously carroty. By adding orange (which is super with carrots: it must be a colour thing!), honey and Moroccan spices, you create something that goes beyond the call of the usual side dish. Serve these with your Sunday roast or with a simply cooked piece of white fish and some chopped, fresh coriander for a special week-night supper.

Heat the butter in a medium-sized lidded pan. Add the orange juice, honey, turmeric, cumin seeds and salt and pepper and bring to the boil. Tip in the carrots and give a good stir. Cover with a lid and reduce the heat.

Cook gently for 12 minutes, stirring occasionally to make sure the liquid has not evaporated and the carrots are not sticking; if they are, add a splash of water to the pan, but the carrots will release their own liquid too, so you shouldn't need to worry. When the carrots have softened and are nicely glazed, they are ready to serve.

Serves 4
Preparation time 5 minutes
Cooking time 15 minutes

30g butter
juice of 2 oranges
1 tablespoon honey
¼ teaspoon ground turmeric
½ teaspoon cumin seeds
sea salt and freshly ground black pepper
500g whole baby Chantilly carrots, washed and leaves trimmed

Mixed vegetables with
CHILLI HONEY BUTTER

Mixed vegetables are one of many things you can use this honey butter for, and I would recommend always having some in the fridge so you can throw a quick meal together. It's spectacular with prawns, steak or corn on the cob, and just as terrific on toast! In this recipe I'm using it with a vibrant collection of mixed veggies – a staple in our household, either for a quick week-night supper with some grilled meat or fish, or as part of your Sunday roast. I challenge you not to become addicted!

Serves 4
Preparation time 10 minutes
Cooking time 10 minutes
Chilling time 1 hour

1 courgette, trimmed, halved and sliced
    lengthways
100g long, thin baby carrots, or 1 large carrot,
    peeled, halved and sliced lengthways
100g broccoli florets
100g baby leeks, halved lengthways
100g green beans, trimmed
1 tablespoon chopped fresh parsley

For the chilli honey butter
125g butter, room temperature
1½ tablespoons honey
1 teaspoon cayenne pepper
a pinch of salt

Mix together the butter, honey, cayenne and salt in a bowl and give it a really good mash with the back of a fork. Lay out a double 30cm piece of clingfilm on your kitchen surface and pile the butter into the centre of it. Roll the clingfilm over the butter and squeeze into a sausage shape. Twist the ends as tightly as possible in opposite directions so you have a neat sausage of chilli honey butter. Pop this into the fridge to chill for at least an hour.

When you're ready to use the butter, cut a couple of slices off the end and slowly melt it in a sauté pan. Tip in the prepared vegetables and sauté over a medium heat for 5 minutes, or until the veggies have softened. Sprinkle over the parsley and serve piping hot.

Purple SPROUTING BROCCOLI *with* STILTON SAUCE

Purple sprouting broccoli is terribly fashionable now, but I know quite a few people still don't really know how to work with it. I remember getting hooked on it after seeing Hugh Fearnley-Whittingstall serve it with a blue cheese sauce. Here's my interpretation.

Melt the butter in a small saucepan. Add the flour and stir over a low heat for one minute, until the mixture foams. Remove from the heat and add the milk, bit by bit. The sauce will thicken almost straight away, but the more milk you add the thinner it will get. If you don't add the milk very slowly it will become lumpy.

Put the pan back on the heat and stir until gently boiling. Boil for 2 minutes, continuing to stir to prevent it catching on the bottom of the pan. Add the cheese and stir until melted. Season with salt and pepper.

Bring a large pan of salted water to the boil. Chuck in the broccoli and boil for 3–4 minutes, or until tender but still retaining some bite. Drain, then transfer to a serving dish. Pour over the Stilton sauce and serve.

Serves 4
Preparation time 10 minutes
Cooking time 10 minutes

20g butter
20g plain flour
300ml milk
150g Stilton cheese, crumbled
sea salt and freshly ground black pepper
500g purple sprouting broccoli, leaves and
    stalks, cut into 10cm lengths

Red cabbage with
APPLES & SULTANAS

There are not many side dishes that stand out as much if not more than the meat or fish you might be serving them with, but a good red cabbage dish that's a little bit sweet and a little bit sour rocks! My Mum's part Polish, and hers is the best I've had. It needs a while to cook, and those who are not big fans of sultanas can simply leave them out. At home we eat this with pork chops, shepherd's pie or venison.

Serves 4
Preparation time 15 minutes
Cooking time 1 hour

2 tablespoons olive oil
2 red onions, thinly sliced
½ large red cabbage (or 1 small one), cored and thinly sliced
150ml red wine vinegar
150ml water
3 tablespoons brown sugar
2 apples, any firm variety, peeled, cored and thinly sliced
50g sultanas
sea salt and freshly ground black pepper

Heat the olive oil in a large pan (I use a wok). Fry the onions gently for 8 minutes, or until they have softened and started to get a golden tinge. Add the cabbage and stir-fry for a further 5 minutes.

Add the vinegar, water and sugar and stir until the sugar has dissolved, then pop a lid on and leave to simmer slowly for 20 minutes.

Now add the apples and sultanas and cook for a further 20 minutes. You may need to check the water level at this stage – when you move the cabbage away with a spoon it should slowly leave a drool of lightly syrupy liquid. You don't want it too dry, but it shouldn't be too wet either.

Season with salt and pepper and serve.

WHY NOT TRY?

Adding pancetta: Add some crisp pancetta at the beginning of cooking for a more savoury version of the dish, as I've done here.

Root vegetable RÖSTIS

A perfect crisp rösti works brilliantly as a side dish, or you can eat it the traditional way as a main course. Röstis can be made with most things, and the addition of bacon, red peppers or spring onions brings them into a new dimension. I have made this one with a mix of root veg and it is dangerously good. Try it with a fried duck breast or even with a fried egg on top.

Parboil the carrots and parsnips.

Preheat the oven to 200ºC/gas 6. Heat 1 tablespoon of olive oil in a non-stick frying pan and throw in the onion. Fry for 5 minutes, until it has softened and started to go golden. Remove from the pan and leave to cool for 5 minutes on some kitchen paper. Meanwhile grate the parboiled carrots and parsnips.

Put the grated potato inside a clean tea towel and squeeze to remove excess water. Tip into a bowl with the carrots, parsnips, onion and thyme. Season really well and mix everything together. Divide into 4 portions and squeeze each one to make a cake shape.

Heat the rest of the oil in a non-stick frying pan. Pop the 4 röstis into the pan and cook over a medium heat for 6–8 minutes, until golden brown and crisp underneath. Flip them over and continue cooking for another 6–8 minutes, until golden on the other side. Pop on to a baking tray, put them into the oven for 5 minutes, and serve.

Makes 4
Preparation time 10 minutes
Cooking time 30 minutes

2 large carrots, peeled
2 large parsnips, peeled
3 tablespoons olive oil
1 onion, peeled and finely chopped
2 large baking potatoes, peeled and grated
a few sprigs of fresh thyme, leaves picked

WHY NOT TRY?

Potato rösti: Swap the parsnips and carrots for another two large baking potatoes and make in the same way.

Teriyaki ASPARAGUS

It's always hard to know what to serve with Asian food, particularly Japanese, but thanks to a lot of the trendy modern Japanese restaurants out there it's becoming easier to find inspiration. There is a restaurant in town where I insist on ordering teriyaki asparagus everytime I go. This teriyaki sauce recipe will make more than you need, but it keeps for ages in the fridge. You can use the same sauce for beef, chicken or salmon. It kicks ass.

Serves 2
Preparation time 5 minutes
Cooking time 5 minutes

8–10 stalks of asparagus, depending on how hungry you are, parboiled for 1 minute
1 tablespoon olive oil
1 teaspoon sesame seeds (I like a mix of white and black), toasted

For the teriyaki sauce
200ml soy sauce (I love Kikkoman)
200ml sake (Japanese rice wine)
2 tablespoons mirin (sweet rice wine)
3 tablespoons sugar

Place all the teriyaki ingredients in a small pan and cook over a low heat until the sugar has melted. Turn up the heat and bring to the boil for 3–5 minutes, or until the sauce has thickened and gone syrupy. Pour into a jug and leave to cool a little.

Heat a griddle pan until smoking. Toss the parboiled asparagus in the oil, then lay them on the griddle. Grill for 1–2 minutes on each side, or until slightly charred and cooked through.

Transfer to a serving plate and pour over some of the sauce. Finish with a sprinkling of toasted sesame seeds.

CURRY, RICE & ALL THINGS SPICE

This is probably the chapter I am most passionate about – spice is where I feel truly comfortable, and I guess you could say it's where my heart is. The recipes are among those I've collected from my travels, friends, family and even some of my favourite restaurants, so they are all very personal to me.

Authenticity is something I really believe in when cooking Asian food. It drives me potty when I see bastardised or even anglicised menus or recipes. The authentic stuff is so good – why mess with it?

I know a lot of people find it easier to reach for the phone to dial for a curry rather than making one themselves, but do have a go. It's no different from making a stew, just uses a few more ingredients, and if it's the ingredients that put you off, it doesn't take long to familiarise yourself with them. I feel as at home with galangal or turmeric as I do with sage and parsley. They are only ingredients – nothing frightening!

A lot of my recipes involve making pastes, which simply means bunging loads of ingredients into a blender. All the work is done by pressing a button, it couldn't be easier.

So next time you're tempted to phone for a curry, stop and give it a try yourself.

Rice Tips & Tricks

★ Avoid easy cook rice – the grains are partially cooked and for some reason end up going a bit furry. You can't beat the real thing!

★ Always rinse your rice before cooking it. This is for two reasons, to clean it and to remove excess starch, which may make it stick.

★ Use a saucepan that's big enough for the rice to be able to steam in, and only fill the water halfway up the pan.

★ Always season your rice by adding a little salt to the water before cooking it. The rice will absorb the salt, which flavours it. It's pretty bland without it!

★ Cover the pot when you bring the rice to a boil and leave the lid on for 5 minutes. This starts off the cooking process.

★ When you switch the heat off to steam the rice, ensure the lid is firmly on so no steam can escape, then keep that lid on for the full 10 minutes.

★ Fluff the cooked rice up with a fork, and be gentle.

★ Never let leftover rice hang about outside the fridge as it can become poisonous. Pop it straight into the fridge once it's cooled.

Cooking RICE

With so many rice cooking techniques out there (every packet seems to say something different), it's no surprise that many people are not sure where they stand. In general, I was cooking really well, but the thing that would keep coming back and haunting me was rice. It's all too easy to get a sludgy rice stew, or rice that's fluffy on the outside and shall we say a little too al dente on the inside! I learnt this trick a while ago in Thailand, while watching a chef work in the hotel we were staying in, and it has not failed me yet. The combination of washing the rice, then boiling it, then steaming it will stay with you for life.

Serves 4
Preparation time 2 minutes
Cooking time 15 minutes

250g rice (either long-grain or basmati), washed under cold water for a minute
enough cold water to cover the rice by 8mm
a pinch of salt

Place the rice in a saucepan and add the water and salt. Place a lid on the pan and bring to the boil. Boil the rice for 5 minutes, then peek under the lid. You want the rice to have swollen but still be firm and surrounded with a little water.

Turn the rice off and leave it to steam for 10 minutes in the water that remains in the pan. The rice will finish cooking in the steam and each grain will remain individual and firm but cooked through.

Take a fork to the rice to fluff it up and serve immediately.

Let's face it – the Thais know their rice.

Fragrant RICE PILAF TO SERVE WITH CURRIES, TAGINES, GRILLS – ANYTHING, IN FACT!

Sometimes you want something more exciting than your usual boiled or steamed rice. My mother makes this amazing rice pilaf that is a variation on Persian rice. We used to have it with grilled kebabs, but I've tried it with curries, tagines, chops, you name it – it's a fantastic accompaniment to anything. It wows at dinner parties, soothes on winter evenings and brightens up family meals. It's just as delicious cold as it is hot, and equally makes a great dish served on its own or as an accompaniment.

Serves 4
Preparation time 10 minutes
Cooking time 40 minutes

30g butter, plus 1 tablespoon extra
2 onions, peeled and thinly sliced
3 garlic cloves, peeled and finely chopped
250g basmati rice
1 cinnamon stick
1 bay leaf
3 or 4 whole cloves
400ml chicken or vegetable stock
100g vermicelli noodles, cooked
sea salt and freshly ground black pepper

Preheat the oven to 200°C/gas 6. Melt the 30g of butter in a casserole, then throw in the onions and cook them really slowly over a lowish heat for 20 minutes, until soft, sweet and caramelised. Add the garlic for the last minute of cooking. Stir in the rice, cinnamon, bay leaf and cloves and coat in the butter for 1 minute. Cover with the stock, pop a lid on the casserole and place in the oven for 10 minutes.

Just before the rice is done, heat the tablespoon of butter in a frying pan until it turns light brown. Stir through the vermicelli noodles until they crisp up a little. Pour the burnt butter and vermicelli into the rice pilaf and give a good stir. The rice should almost be cooked at this stage. Place the rice pan in the oven, uncovered, and cook for another 5 minutes so that the top of the rice crisps up. Serve immediately.

WHY NOT TRY?

Pomegranate fragrant rice: Add the seeds of 1 pomegranate to the rice at the end of cooking.

Lemon rice: Swap the cloves for 5 curry leaves, 1 teaspoon mustard seeds, ½ teaspoon ground cumin and the zest and juice of 1 lemon.

SPICE TIPS & TRICKS

Try to refresh your spice cupboard every 6 months. Spices lose their freshness, taking on a dusty taste, and you will not get the same impact if they are stale.

* Store spices in airtight jars, away from sunlight.

* Store aromatic spices, such as ginger, chillies, lemongrass, lime leaves and herbs, in the fridge, or they will dry out and lose their freshness.

* If grinding your own spices, use the same volume of whole spices as you would ground.

* Some spices – most notably garam masala – should be added at the end of cooking.

SPICE

* It is important to 'cook your spices out' by toasting them in oil over a low heat for a minute or two. This will awaken the flavours and really bring them to life.

* If creating your own recipes, be careful not to over-spice your food. Remember, it's easy to add more spice at the end of cooking but impossible to take it away.

* If you have any excess curry paste left over, it will last for 10 days in the fridge and freezes brilliantly. And on the subject of freezing, most curries freeze fantastically well too!

MY PERFECT SPICE CUPBOARD

Allspice
Black peppercorns
Caraway
Cayenne pepper
Chilli flakes
Chilli powder
Chinese 5-spice powder
Cinnamon (both sticks and ground)
Cloves
Coriander (seeds and ground)
Cumin (seeds and ground)
Curry powder (I love a proper Indian Madras powder)
Fennel seeds

Fenugreek (I think ground is a bit easier)
Nutmeg (whole – always grate it fresh)
Onion seeds
Paprika
Mustard powder (the good old English stuff)
Mustard seeds
Saffron
Smoked paprika
Star anise
Turmeric (ground)
White pepper (ground)

FRESH OR DRIED?

I would never normally suggest using dried herbs, but freeze-dried kaffir lime leaves and curry leaves are a great alternative, as the fresh variety are quite difficult to get hold of.

I also keep dried chipotle chillies, dried ancho chillies, dried tamarind and shrimp paste, among other weird and wonderful things from my travels.

WHOLE OR GROUND?

Arguably it is always better to use whole spices and grind them yourself, but I can accept that day to day that could be quite a feat. If you really want to do this, invest in a rough-textured pestle and mortar or a good coffee grinder.

In some cases whole spices are used to infuse flavour and don't need grinding at all, or partially crushed spices are used to make a spice crust, so I do think it's important to have a variety of whole and ground spices in your perfect spice cupboard.

Chicken in WEEDS

Don't be put off by the name – it's not really cooked in weeds! Just tons of coriander, which is almost used as a vegetable. I can't take responsibility for this recipe, it's one of my mum's, and she honed it from a Madhur Jaffrey recipe many moons ago. We were brought up on this stuff, as it's so mild that it's great for kids. It's tinged with lemon and ginger, which make it quite user-friendly. When asked what we wanted for dinner as kids you could bet your bottom dollar you'd hear me and my sisters screaming in unison, 'Chicken in weeds!'

Put the ginger and the 4 tablespoons of water into a blender and blitz until you have a paste. Heat the oil in a large heavy-bottomed pan and brown the chicken in batches. Scoop it out with a slotted spoon and leave to rest on a plate while you get on with the rest of the recipe.

Add the onion to the pan and cook slowly for about 10 minutes, or until softened and turning golden. Add the garlic for the last few minutes of cooking. Pour over the ginger paste and stir-fry until starting to brown. Add the fresh coriander, chilli, spices and salt to the pan and cook for a further minute.

Pop the chicken back into the pan with any juices from the plate. Add the water or stock and the lemon juice, put a lid on the pan and cook for 15 minutes. Turn the chicken, then put the lid back on and cook for a further 15 minutes. If the sauce is too thin, cook with the lid off until it's thickened up a bit. The chicken should be melting off the bone when it's ready. Serve with rice.

Serves 4
Preparation time 15 minutes
Cooking time 45 minutes

5cm piece of fresh root ginger, peeled and chopped
300ml water (or chicken stock), plus 4 tablespoons
4 tablespoons vegetable oil
8 chicken thighs, on the bone, skin removed
1 onion, peeled and finely chopped
5 garlic cloves, peeled and finely chopped
200g fresh coriander, finely chopped
1 long green chilli, finely chopped
½ teaspoon cayenne pepper
2 teaspoons ground cumin
1 teaspoon ground coriander
½ teaspoon ground turmeric
1 teaspoon sea salt
2 tablespoons lemon juice

Thai GREEN CURRY –
THE *genuine article*

I have looked up many Thai green curry recipes in my time and I'm not going to beat about the bush – my obsession with authenticity is going to have you making a trip to your local Asian supermarket. You will need to go there for the lime leaves (which freeze, so buy loads), aubergines and Thai basil. If you're less worried about being authentic, put in whichever veggies you fancy, but the best ones to use are peas, beans or asparagus.

Serves 4
Preparation time 20 minutes
Cooking time 10 minutes

4 boneless chicken breasts, sliced
8 green aubergines, quartered
2 handfuls of spring pea aubergines, picked off their stems
2 x 400g tins of coconut milk
2 tablespoons Thai fish sauce
1 tablespoon palm or brown sugar
2 lime leaves, sliced
1 red chilli, sliced
100g carton of coconut cream
Thai basil, to serve

For the paste
2 long green chillies
10 green bird's-eye chillies
1 tablespoon chopped lemongrass
3 shallots, peeled and chopped
8 garlic cloves, peeled and chopped
a small bunch of fresh coriander (with roots if possible)
½ teaspoon ground cumin
2 teaspoons ground coriander
½ teaspoon white pepper (you know, the old fashioned stuff that makes you sneeze – it's everywhere in Thailand and really distinctive in their cooking)
3 lime leaves, chopped
2 teaspoons of shrimp paste (you can buy this in the supermarket now)
1 teaspoon salt
3 tablespoons groundnut or vegetable oil

Put all the paste ingredients into a blender and blitz until smooth. Heat a wok and add the paste to the pan. Stir-fry for 1 minute, or until the room fills with a gorgeous aroma, then add the chicken. Stir to coat the chicken in the paste, then add all the aubergines.

Pour over the coconut milk, add the fish sauce, sugar, lime leaves and chilli and leave to simmer for about 7 minutes, or until the chicken and aubergines are cooked through and the sauce has thickened a little.

Pour into a serving dish and swirl in the coconut cream and some Thai basil leaves. Serve with rice.

WHY NOT TRY?

Prawn Thai green curry: Substitute the chicken with 24 peeled raw king prawns.

Vegetarian Thai green curry: Substitute the chicken with 200g of cubed firm tofu, 100g of broccoli florets and 12 pieces of baby corn.

Sunny's (LEGENDARY) CHICKEN *curry*

Sunny is my pal. She's British but her family hails from the Punjab, in northern India. She cooks a mean chicken curry – it's proper! It was the first curry she was taught to cook when she was eighteen, and true to form the curry has been passed down from generation to generation. I once asked her what the trick was to curry-making and she said it's just about giving the curry some love, letting it have the time it needs for all the flavours to develop, and curry is best served a day or two after making it. I'll take my hat off to that too, but don't feel like you can't eat it the day it's made. It'll still be darned delicious! Notice how a lot of the work is put in at the beginning with the onions – that's where you're going to build that deep base flavour. It's worth it, though. You're getting the real deal.

Bring a full kettle to the boil. Heat the ghee in a large deep pan. Add the onions and sauté for about 5 minutes until slightly golden, then add the salt and cumin seeds and toast for a further 2 minutes. Add the garlic, ginger and chillies and cook for a further 3 minutes, until everything is nicely golden.

Turn the heat up and add enough boiling water to just cover the onions. Let them simmer slowly, stirring occasionally, until the water has reduced almost completely (be careful not to let it burn!). Keep adding water for around 10–15 minutes until the onions are mushy. You are looking to make this into a paste, so by all means go at it with a potato masher.

Turn the heat down to medium, add some more boiling water (again just covering the paste), then add the spices and stir. Cover the pan (as it starts to splatter in all directions!) and simmer for about 5–10 minutes. Add the tomatoes. At this stage, it should be quite soupy, so if it's too watery, keep simmering it until it's reduced.

Add the chicken and give everything a good stir. Pour over the 500ml stock or water, making sure there is enough to just cover the chicken, and leave to simmer on a low heat, stirring it every now and then, for 40 minutes.

Finally stir in the coriander, check the seasoning and serve. In the words of Sunny – JOB DONE!

Serves 4
Preparation time 20 minutes
Cooking time 1 hour 20 minutes

2 tablespoons ghee (ghee is clarified butter, but regular butter would be fine)
2 to 3 large onions, peeled and chopped
1 teaspoon sea salt
1 tablespoon cumin seeds
4–6 garlic cloves, peeled and crushed (depending on how big a garlic fan you are)
3cm piece of fresh root ginger, peeled and grated
1–2 long green chillies, finely chopped (depending on how hot you like your curry)
1 tablespoon turmeric
1 tablespoon garam masala
1 tablespoon ground coriander
1 teaspoon chilli powder
1 teaspoon Madras curry powder
200g tinned chopped tomatoes
8 chicken thighs, on the bone, skin removed
500ml chicken stock or water
a generous handful of fresh coriander, chopped (use the roots too – tons of flavour)
sea salt and freshly ground black pepper

Afghan YOGHURT CHICKEN

The Afghan Kitchen restaurant in Islington sells one of the best curries in London – a simple yoghurt curry, the recipe for which has been a carefully guarded secret of theirs for many years. Their tight-lipped silence only made me more curious, so I put my conjuring gloves on and here, after years of refining, is my version. I hope you'll agree I've done a good job.

Heat the oil in a medium, lidded casserole pan. Brown the chicken in batches, then remove from the pan with a slotted spoon and set aside. In the remaining fat left in the pan, cook the onion over a low heat for 8 minutes, or until it has softened and taken on a lightly caramelised tinge. For the last minute of cooking add the garlic and chilli.

Now tip in the spices and toast them over a low heat for a minute. Add the yoghurt, chicken and a splash of water to the pan and give it a good stir. Add the chopped herbs and a little salt and pepper, stir, then cover with a lid and let it poach away for 20 minutes. The trick to this curry is slow cooking, so you just want it to bubble gently. The curry is ready when the chicken is cooked through and tender and the sauce has thickened. Don't be worried if the sauce looks a little curdled – it's caused by the yoghurt, but you can add a splash of water if you like. Serve with rice.

Serves 4
Preparation time 10 minutes
Cooking time 40 minutes

1 tablespoon groundnut or vegetable oil
8 boneless chicken thighs, skin removed, each cut into 4 pieces
1 onion, peeled and finely chopped
5 garlic cloves, peeled and chopped
1 green chilli, finely chopped
1 teaspoon ground coriander
1 teaspoon ground cumin
3 cardamom pods, crushed
1 teaspoon hot paprika
500g Greek yoghurt
a small bunch of fresh coriander, finely chopped
a small bunch of fresh mint, finely chopped
sea salt and freshly ground black pepper

Lamb MASSAMAN CURRY

For those who are a bit wimpy when it comes to all things spicy, a lamb massaman curry is perfect. It's really mild, and more like a flavourful and comforting stew than a fierce curry, but it's also quite complex because of the caramelised shallots, garlic and sweet spices. A pretty impressive dinner-party dish for you to wow your guests with your knowledge of Asian flavours.

Serves 4
Preparation time 15 minutes
Cooking time 1 hour 45 minutes

500g lamb neck fillet, cut into 3cm cubes
2 x 400g tins of coconut milk
400ml lamb or chicken stock
2 tablespoons brown sugar
8 smallish waxy new potatoes
sea salt and freshly ground black pepper
3 tablespoons peanuts, toasted and crushed
rice and fresh coriander, to serve

For the curry paste
4 shallots, peeled and sliced
5 garlic cloves, peeled
2 red chillies
3cm piece of fresh root ginger, peeled and
    sliced
2 stalks of lemongrass, outer leaves removed,
    then chopped
1 tablespoon ground coriander
1 tablespoon ground cumin
½ teaspoon nutmeg, grated
½ teaspoon ground cinnamon
¼ teaspoon ground cloves
4 cardamom pods, crushed
2 tablespoons Thai fish sauce
1 teaspoon shrimp paste (from the international
    section of the supermarket)
3 tablespoons groundnut oil

Put all the paste ingredients into a blender and blitz for 30 seconds until smooth. Heat a wok (one with a lid), pour in the paste and stir-fry for 1 minute to awaken the flavours. Add the lamb and stir-fry on a high heat for a good 5 minutes, until the meat is coated in the paste. You want to try to get some colour on the meat, so make sure the heat is quite high, but not so high that the paste burns.

Add the coconut milk, stock and brown sugar, then pop the lid on top and leave to bubble away very gently for 45 minutes. Add the potatoes, cover again, and carry on cooking for a further 45 minutes. The curry is ready when the lamb is meltingly tender and the potatoes are cooked through. Season with salt and pepper, and serve with rice. Scatter peanuts and fresh coriander on top of the curry.

Muttar PANEER

I cannot even remember the first time I had muttar paneer, but what I can tell you is that it has to be one of the most delicious dishes, veggie or not. The paneer cheese has a texture like tofu, although it is more often compared with cottage cheese. The peas burst with each mouthful, and the mild curry base is so flexible you can use it with whatever you like.

Make the paste by whizzing together the oil, onion, ginger, garlic and spices in a blender.

Heat a wok or pan, then add the oil, a tablespoon at a time. When it's hot, fry the paneer until golden brown. Scoop out with a slotted spoon and set aside to drain on some kitchen paper.

Add the paste and fry for about 5 minutes, or until it starts to brown a little and the room fills with a spicy aroma. Add the tomatoes and stock and simmer for 10 minutes until thickened. Add the paneer and the peas and cook for 5 minutes, then season to taste and serve with naan bread.

Swap the peas for a bag of baby spinach and you've got a great saag paneer!

Serves 4
Preparation time 10 minutes
Cooking time 25 minutes

2 tablespoons vegetable oil
250g paneer (Indian cheese, found in the cheese section of the supermarket), cut into chunks
4 very ripe tomatoes, roughly chopped
300ml vegetable stock
300g frozen peas
sea salt and freshly ground black pepper
naan bread, to serve

For the curry paste
2 tablespoons vegetable oil
1 onion, peeled and chopped
3cm piece of fresh root ginger, peeled and chopped
4 garlic cloves, peeled and chopped
a pinch of garam masala
2 teaspoons ground turmeric
½ teaspoon cayenne pepper

Chicken katsu CURRY

Anyone who is into Japanese food knows that katsu curry is wickedly wonderful. What makes it stand out from other curries is that the meat is breaded and fried before having a luxurious silky curry sauce slathered all over it. I've used chicken here, but I have also eaten this made with juicy king prawns or with pork tenderloin, both equally delicious. Offering crunch, spice and sauce, this is real comfort food.

Serves 4
Preparation time 15 minutes
Cooking time 35 minutes

100g flour, seasoned with lots of salt and
    pepper
1 free-range egg, beaten lightly
200g Japanese panko breadcrumbs
4 boneless chicken breasts
100ml groundnut or vegetable oil
steamed rice and salad to serve

For the curry sauce
1 tablespoon groundnut or vegetable oil
1 onion, peeled and chopped
5 whole garlic cloves, peeled
2 carrots, peeled and chopped
2 tablespoons plain flour
1 tablespoon medium curry powder
600ml chicken stock
2 teaspoons honey
1 tablespoon soy sauce
1 bay leaf
½ teaspoon garam masala

To make the sauce, heat the oil in a small pan. Add the onion and garlic and sauté for 2 minutes, then throw in the carrots and cook slowly for 10 minutes with the lid on, giving the odd stir occasionally. You want to sweat the vegetables until softened and starting to caramelise.

Stir in the flour and curry powder and cook for a minute. Slowly pour in the stock bit by bit until combined (do this gradually to avoid getting lumps). Add the honey, soy sauce and bay leaf and bring to the boil, then reduce the heat to a slow simmer and cook for 20 minutes. The sauce will have thickened and taken on all of the flavours, although you still need it to have a pouring consistency. Add the garam masala, then pass the sauce through a sieve. (Some people might like a chunky sauce, so feel free not to strain it, but I prefer it nice and smooth.)

Now prepare the chicken. Lay the seasoned flour, egg and breadcrumbs on separate plates. Coat the chicken in the flour, then dip into the egg and finally into the breadcrumbs.

Heat the oil in a frying pan and fry the breaded chicken breasts for 5 minutes on each side, or until golden and cooked through. Remove from the pan with a slotted spoon and leave to drain on kitchen paper. Slice the chicken diagonally and serve with the sauce drizzled over, steamed rice and salad.

Serve it with Japanese pickles for a really authentic katsu curry.

Nasi GORENG

This dish is more special than any other fried rice I can think of because it has so many different textures and flavours. In Malaysia you will find it made with tiny dried anchovies, but they are pretty hard to come by over here. In their place I have used crisp shallots, which give the same element of crunch; as a flavour of the East they sit very comfortably in there. The fabulous nasi goreng paste has the most wonderful smell. There will be more than you need, but just store it for another time. Wok and roll!

Serves 4
Preparation time 20 minutes
Cooking time 30 minutes

2 mackerel fillets, sliced in half widthways
sea salt and freshly ground black pepper
4 tablespoons sunflower oil
6 large shallots, peeled and thinly sliced
1 boneless chicken breast, thinly sliced
200g small cooked prawns
250g basmati rice, cooked and cooled
1 tablespoon light soy sauce
4 spring onions, sliced lengthways
4 large free-range eggs
5cm piece of cucumber, quartered lengthways
   and sliced

For the nasi goreng paste
3 tablespoons groundnut oil
4 large garlic cloves, peeled and roughly
   chopped
2 large shallots, peeled and roughly chopped
15g roasted, unsalted peanuts
3 red chillies, roughly chopped
3cm piece of fresh root ginger, peeled and
   roughly chopped
1 tablespoon tomato purée
½ teaspoon blachan (dried shrimp paste) or, if
   you're stuck, 1 tablespoon Thai fish sauce
1 tablespoon ketap manis (sweet soy sauce)

First make the nasi goreng paste: put all the paste ingredients into a food processor and blend until smooth. Preheat the grill to high and season the mackerel on both sides with salt and pepper. Lay the fish on a lightly oiled baking tray or the rack of a grill pan, and grill for 4 minutes on each side.

Pour the sunflower oil into a wok. Add the shallots and fry over a medium heat until crisp and golden brown. Lift them out with a slotted spoon and leave to drain on kitchen paper.

Add 2 tablespoons of the nasi goreng paste and stir-fry for 2 minutes. Add the chicken and prawns and stir-fry for 5 minutes, or until golden brown. Add the cooked rice and stir-fry over a high heat for another 2 minutes, until it has heated through. Add the fried shallots and stir-fry for another minute.

Add the soy sauce and most of the spring onions, then toss together well and divide between serving plates. Quickly fry the eggs in a frying pan. Serve each portion of nasi goreng with a fried egg, a piece of mackerel and some cucumber slices, and sprinkle with the rest of the spring onions.

FISH & SHELLFISH

One of the questions I often get asked as a cook is what would be my last supper, and everything that springs to mind for me involves some kind of seafood. I love tuna sashimi more than anything else in the world, and have never been known to turn down lobster or crab if it's on the menu. There is something so opulent about it, and I can't resist delicious food that you have to really muck in with to eat.

And then there's the lightness of fish, which always seems to make me feel pure after eating it. Even with battered fish and chips, I am somehow able to justify the naughty part of it because it feels so light.

Fish always evokes memories of the beach for me, too. A lot of the dishes in this chapter are inspired by holidays by the sea, which I think is the best place to start when devising a seafood recipe. Its natural home. One thing we should think about is sustainability. It's always a good idea to ask your fishmonger or find out from your supermarket if the fish you are eating is MSC-certified (guaranteed sustainable by the Marine Stewardship Council). Do also check out their website (www.msc.org).

For those of you who (like a whole bunch of us) are a bit scared of cooking fish but love to eat it when you're out these recipes are completely user-friendly and most of them can be thrown together in a tick. Fish is one of the easiest and tastiest fast foods to get into – so don't be afraid, dive in!

★ ☆ TIPS & TRICKS ☆ ★

Frozen or fresh? For me there is no contest, fresh is best, but you will find that a lot of fish is frozen on the boats and defrosted for the fish counters in the supermarkets. If you go to a proper fishmonger's they will be able to tell you what has or hasn't been frozen beforehand. It is rare for things like prawns to be fresh, and when they are they are very expensive. Get your fishmonger to prepare the fish for you. A good fishmonger will be happy to help and it will take them just seconds to do what would take you many minutes. (There are some skills better left to someone else. You wouldn't be expected to butcher a cow, so why fillet a fish?)

FRESHNESS

* The freshest fish is bought from the markets that day. No matter how convenient, you will not get the best fish from a supermarket. Find a local fishmonger you can trust and buy your fish from them.

* Never buy fish on a Monday. The fish markets are closed on Sundays and Mondays, so the fish will be three days old. In fish terms, that's well and truly past it.

* Fish is only fresh for 2 days, but is at its best on the day you buy it, so try not to buy too much at once.

* Make sure the fish has clear glassy eyes, bright red, healthy-looking gills and smells clean (it should not smell even remotely 'fishy').

* Fresh fish should be firm. The closer to rigor mortis, the firmer it will be. A really fresh fish will stand up by itself if you hold it up by the tail. As it loses freshness, it becomes floppy.

* A fresh fish has neat, undamaged scales that will require some effort to remove.

FISH COOKERY

* Season fish before cooking, as salt draws out moisture, making it extra juicy and easier to brown.

* When pan-frying, griddling or grilling fish with its skin on, always lay it skin side down in the hot oil first. Cook the fish three-quarters of the way through on the skin side, then turn it over for the last quarter of its cooking time to finish it off.

* However, when cooking fish with skin on in the oven, lay it skin side up to ensure it's golden and crisp.

* When pan-frying fish, coat it with a little seasoned flour so that it becomes crisp.

* Be very careful when turning fish over, so that it doesn't break up. Use the correct utensils, such as a fish slice, to make it easier.

* If fish is dry, it has been overcooked. Most fish should be cooked so that the middle is a little translucent and not totally cooked through.

* When grilling or griddling fish, coat it in oil first to prevent it sticking and drying out.

HOW TO SKIN FISH

To skin a raw fish fillet, lay the fish skin side down on a board. Start at the tail end and with two fingers coated in salt, hold the tail. With a sharp (and if possible flexible) knife, cut through the thinnest part of the flesh to the skin. Angle the knife very slightly down so that the edge points towards the skin. Hold the skin tightly, and carefully slide the knife all the way down the fillet, using a gentle sawing motion. This should be quite easy, almost as if you are pulling the skin off the fish. If you are using individual fillets, do the same but make a nick along the edge of the fillet and carve the skin off that way.

HOW TO PEEL PRAWNS

To peel a prawn, first detach the head from the body by finding the little joint that separates the two pieces and twisting them apart. Hold the prawn with your thumbs in between its legs and gently pull apart. The shell will peel off really easily. You can remove the whole shell or leave the bottom part covering the tail. Now, using a knife, slice along the back of the prawn to reveal a black thread, or vein. This is the prawn's guts, so you need to get rid of it, a process known as deveining. Give the prawns a wash and you're ready to go!

HOW TO PREPARE A SQUID

Clean squid by gently pulling the head and tentacles away from the body. Pull out the clear backbone (quill) from inside the body and discard the entrails. Cut the tentacles from the head just below the eyes, then throw the head away. Remove the side wings and the fine membrane from the body. Rinse the body, tentacles and wings thoroughly and pat dry with kitchen paper. Cut the squid body down the centre so that it will open out flat, and slice the body and wings into 5mm-wide strips.

FISH

HOW TO PREPARE MUSSELS (& CLAMS)

Scrub the mussels, tug away any hairy beards and check scrupulously for any broken shells or dead mussels. To do this, take any open mussels and knock them gently against the kitchen surface. If they close quickly, the mussels are alive, but if they remain open the mussel has died and they should be discarded. Once the mussels are cooked, discard any that remain firmly shut, as these will also have been dead before cooking. People get so scared about cooking mussels at home, but it's a simple formula and if you stick to it there is no going wrong.

HOW TO SHUCK OYSTERS

To start with, give your oysters a good scrub to get rid of any mud or sand. As with mussels or clams, check they are alive by seeing if they are tightly closed. Hold the oysters in the palm of your hand with a towel to avoid them slipping. Work over a bowl to catch all the juices. Position the oyster in your hand with the cup side down – so that its curved shell faces down and its flatter side faces up.

Insert a paring or oyster knife between the shells, near the hinge. Twist the knife so that the muscles are detached, then remove the top shell. Scrape the meat from the top shell into the bottom shell. Use the knife to cut the oyster from the bottom shell, or serve it on the half shell. Hey presto – you have your oysters.

I love my oysters served with a dressing made with 1 shallot, finely chopped, mixed with 30ml of Cabernet Sauvignon vinegar and left to infuse for an hour. I drizzle each oyster with a spoonful of the shallot vinegar, then give a good dash of Tabasco on top for spice.

★ ☆ Batter Tips & Tricks ☆ ★

✳ Make sure the oil or fat you are cooking your battered fish in is really hot – this is particularly necessary for deep-frying.

✳ Don't over-beat your batter otherwise it can get tough.

✳ Keep your batter quite cold. It tends to set better and become crisper.

✳ Other than tempura batter, most batter improves if rested for half an hour.

TEMPURA BATTER
Makes 285ml

The lightest and crispest of batters, this works fantastically well with prawns, fish and vegetables. It also makes the most incredible onion rings.

Preparation time 5 minutes

85g plain flour
1 tablespoon cornflour
½ teaspoon sea salt
200ml ice-cold sparkling water

Mix together the flour, cornflour, salt and sparkling water in a bowl. Do not over-mix it. It is better that it is a bit lumpy than over-mixed and totally smooth. You also need to ensure that the water is ice cold. Add some ice cubes if you're worried it's not cold enough.

BEER BATTER
Makes 285ml

You cannot do better than a good old English beer batter. The marriage of beer batter and light white fish is something every Brit should be truly proud of. Team it with some homemade chips and I'm in heaven.

Preparation time 5 minutes

110g self-raising flour
½ teaspoon salt
150ml ice-cold beer or ale

Beat together the flour, salt and beer until the mixture becomes a smooth batter that's free from lumps.

★ ☆ Deep-Frying ☆ ★

Fry everything in small batches. Do not fry too much at once. Always have a pan lid free so that if in the worst case scenario the oil boils over and causes a fire you can put it out.

* Pour enough light vegetable, sunflower or corn oil into either a deep-fat fryer or a large saucepan so it comes one third of the way up the pan. You ideally need a pan that is deep enough to deal with 8cm of oil. Heat the oil. If you have a thermometer it needs to reach 190°C, but you can test that the oil is ready by dropping in a piece of bread – it should brown in 20 seconds.

* Dip whatever you're deep-frying into the batter, shaking off any excess, and fry until golden and crisp. Make sure you fry everything in small batches to avoid the oil bubbling over or the pan getting too full. You can gently move whatever you're frying with a slotted spoon to make sure it gets evenly cooked. Remove with a slotted spoon and drain on kitchen paper.

* To keep things crisp and warm when you are frying in batches, heat the oven to 150°C/gas 2 and line a baking sheet with greaseproof paper. Place each batch on the baking sheet after it's been cooked to keep it warm in the oven, but leave the door open to keep it crisp.

Chateaubriand OF TUNA *with* TOMATO HOLLANDAISE & ZUCCHINI FRITTI

There is nothing sexier than sharing your food, and bringing a whole piece of fish or meat to the table to carve has a real wow factor. The tomato hollandaise adds piquancy to the dish, and you will not be able to get enough of the little fried matchsticks of courgette. If available, fry a few courgette flowers in the same way.

Serves 2
Preparation time 10 minutes
Cooking time 20 minutes

300g freshest tuna loin, in one large even piece
sea salt and freshly ground black pepper
1 teaspoon fennel seeds
1 teaspoon coriander seeds
¼ teaspoon dried chilli flakes
1 tablespoon olive oil

For the tomato hollandaise sauce
1½ tablespoons cider vinegar
1 mandarin orange, juiced (a lemon or lime would also be fine)
2 large free-range egg yolks
150g butter, melted and still hot
1 tomato, seeded and chopped
1 teaspoon chopped fresh chervil

For the zucchini fritti
200ml olive or vegetable oil
100g plain flour
1 teaspoon sea salt
½ teaspoon white pepper
3 green courgettes, cut into thin neat matchsticks

Preheat the oven to 200°C/gas 6. Lay the tuna on a board and season with salt and pepper. Place the spices in a pestle and mortar or a coffee grinder and grind until broken up. Mix the spices in a bowl with the olive oil, then rub the spice mix all over the tuna to form a crust. Heat an ovenproof roasting pan on the hob and brown the tuna for 1 minute on each side. Finish in the oven for 5 minutes, then remove and leave to rest, covered, for 5 minutes.

To make the tomato hollandaise, place the vinegar and mandarin juice in a pan and bring to the boil. Reduce until there is just 1 or 2 teaspoons of liquid left in the pan, then pour into a food processor. Add the egg yolks and start to whiz. Very, very slowly add the hot, melted butter, dribble by dribble. The dressing will become quite thick if you are patient. This whole process can take as long as 10 minutes, so you really must do it as slowly as you can.

To make the zucchini fritti, pour enough oil into a deep but narrow pan to come one-third of the way up the sides, and heat it until hot enough to fry in (a good way of testing this is to drop a small piece of bread into the oil; if it turns golden-brown in 20–25 seconds the oil is ready – any faster and it is too hot; any slower and it's not hot enough). Mix the flour, salt and white pepper together. Coat the courgette matchsticks in the flour mixture, dust them off a little and drop half of them into the oil. Deep-fry for 30–40 seconds, tuning once, then remove, drain on kitchen paper and repeat with the other half.

To serve, lay the tuna on a chopping board, place the courgettes in a pile next to the tuna and pour the hollandaise into a small bowl.

Pan-fried plaice with
PRAWN, LIME & CHILLI BUTTER

I've always found the delicate flakiness of plaice to be such a treat that it seems a shame we are more often drawn to the more obvious charms of salmon and cod. It's one of the easiest fish to work with and tastes marvellous. I came across a similar dish to this while on holiday in Cornwall, and was so inspired – fantastic fish and the best of British produce, with the flavours of Thailand running through it.

Toss the plaice fillets in enough seasoned flour to coat them evenly but thinly. Heat the oil in a frying pan and add the 1 tablespoon of butter. When it starts to foam, lay the fish fillets in the pan, skin side down. Pan-fry for 2–3 minutes on each side, or until the fish is crisp and golden on the outside, but nicely opaque in the middle (you may need to do this in two batches). Remove from the pan and place on a piece of kitchen paper to drain.

Tip out the oil, wipe the pan with a piece of kitchen paper, then add the 80g of butter. Once it starts to foam, tip in the garlic and chilli and sauté them for 1 minute or until the garlic is cooked. Add the prawns to the pan and fry for a further minute. Finally add the coriander, lime juice and seasoning.

Lay a plaice fillet on each plate and cover with a couple of spoonfuls of the prawn and butter sauce.

Serves 4
Preparation time 10 minutes
Cooking time 10 minutes

4 plaice fillets, skin on
50g plain flour, seasoned with salt and pepper
2 tablespoons olive oil
80g butter, plus 1 tablespoon
3 garlic cloves, peeled and finely chopped
1 red chilli, seeded and finely chopped
200g small cooked peeled prawns
a small bunch of fresh coriander, finely
    chopped
juice of 1 lime
sea salt and freshly ground black pepper

Black cod with PLUM MISO

Black cod and miso was originally the signature dish at swanky London restaurant Nobu, but now it seems that every Japanese restaurant is giving it a go. The salty sweetness of the miso sauce marries beautifully with the flaky white cod. I've made it my own by adding a little plum wine to give a fruity tinge.

Serves 4
Preparation time 20 minutes
Marinating time 1 hour
Cooking time 10 minutes

100ml sake (Japanese rice wine)
100ml mirin (sweet rice wine)
100ml plum wine
400g white miso
225g golden caster sugar
4 x 125g fillets of black cod (if you can't find black cod, use white cod or any other flaky white fish, such as red snapper)
2 tablespoons groundnut oil

Pour the sake, mirin and plum wine into a pan and heat until the mixture begins to boil. Turn down the heat, then add the miso and sugar. Stir until the sugar has completely dissolved. Remove from the heat and cool.

Put the black cod into a bowl and cover with three-quarters of the marinade, reserving a little for garnish. Cover the bowl with clingfilm and refrigerate for a good hour.

Preheat the oven to 200°C/gas 6. Wipe any excess marinade from the cod and place in a roasting pan with the oil. Cook for 10 minutes.

Place a piece of cod on each plate. Dot or drizzle the remaining marinade around the plate and serve immediately.

WHY NOT TRY?

Black cod and miso: Simply remove the plum wine and up the sake content by another 100ml to make the classic black cod and miso.

Five-spice salted CHILLI SQUID

I can't go into a Vietnamese restaurant without ordering crispy salted chilli squid, which knocks spots off regular calamari. I learnt the little trick of adding Chinese five-spice powder from a chef on London's Kingsland Road, a prominent Vietnamese area. Five-spice isn't traditional, but it does make it really aromatic and gives it a sweeter finish.

In a large bowl, combine the flour, cornflour, Chinese five-spice, chilli powder and salt. Add the squid rings and tentacles, and toss to coat, shaking off any excess flour.

Heat the oil in a large pan or wok big enough to deep-fry in (see page 109). Add half the squid and deep-fry for about 1 minute, or until just tender and beginning to colour. Remove with a slotted spoon and drain well on kitchen paper. Repeat the process with the remaining squid.

In a wok or frying pan, heat another tablespoon of oil. Add the garlic and fry for about 30 seconds, then add the chilli and fry for a further 30 seconds. Finally, add the spring onions and fry for another 30 seconds. Remove with a slotted spoon.

Arrange the squid on a platter and garnish with the fried garlic, chillies and spring onions. Serve immediately with lemon wedges.

Serves 4
Preparation time 15 minutes
Cooking time 5 minutes

50g plain flour
1 tablespoon cornflour
1 teaspoon Chinese five-spice powder
1 teaspoon hot chilli powder
1 tablespoon sea salt
600g whole squid, cleaned and prepared, bodies cut into rings (see page 107)
vegetable oil, for deep-frying
3 garlic cloves, peeled and finely chopped
2 large red chillies, cut into rings
2 tablespoons sliced spring onion
lemon wedges, to serve

Grilled fish with
CHILLI & MANGO SAUCE

For those of you who have been to Thailand, or any part of South East Asia for that matter, and spent time at beach restaurants, this is a dish that will bring back a flood of memories. The sauce is a prime example of the whole Thai salty, spicy, sweet, sour thing, and while I think the sauce is perfectly balanced, by all means play around with it. If you want it hotter add more chilli, a bit sweeter add more sugar… If you're squeamish you can swap the whole fish for fish fillets. I've gone for sea bass, but the sauce works beautifully with any fish really.

Serves 2
Preparation time 20 minutes
Cooking time 20 minutes

1 medium-sized sea bass, snapper or grey mullet, gutted and scaled
2 tablespoons Thai fish sauce
3 tablespoons shao hsing wine or sherry
3 garlic cloves, finely chopped
a handful of fresh coriander, chopped
2 tablespoons soy sauce
2 tablespoons Thai fish sauce
2 limes, juiced
1 fresh red chilli, chopped
½ firm mango (green – under-ripe – mangoes are great if you can find them), peeled and cut into matchsticks
200ml water
1 teaspoon tamarind paste (available at Indian food stores or the specialist aisle in supermarkets)
2 teaspoons brown sugar
1 teaspoon cornflour, mixed with 2 tablespoons of water
a handful of fresh coriander, leaves picked, to garnish

Heat a grill on a high heat. Using a sharp serrated knife, and holding the fish firmly in front of you, make 3 or 4 cuts on each side of it. This allows the marinade and sauce to penetrate. Put the fish into a bowl, pour the fish sauce over and leave to marinate for 5–10 minutes.

Put all the remaining ingredients except the cornflour and the coriander into a saucepan. Place over a medium heat and bring gently to a simmer. Pour in the cornflour mixture and stir until thickened. Keep the pan on minimum heat until the fish is cooked, or cover and keep warm.

Grill the fish for 8 minutes on each side or until crisp and golden on the outside but firm and flaky when pushed in its meatiest part. Place on a serving platter and pour over the sauce. Finally sprinkle with the coriander and serve – for me the only way is with steamed rice and pak choi.

Mussels WITH CIDER & *cream*

Here I've taken the French way of cooking mussels and given it a British twist. Delicious!

Serves 4
Preparation time 15 minutes
Cooking time 15 minutes

2 tablespoons butter
3 medium-sized shallots, finely chopped
3 garlic cloves, peeled and finely chopped
500ml dry cider
3kg mussels, cleaned (see page 107)
100ml double cream
sea salt and freshly ground black pepper
2 tablespoons finely chopped fresh parsley
crusty bread, to serve

Heat the butter in a large deep pan. Add the shallots and cook for 3–5 minutes or until softened. For the last minute of cooking, add the garlic.

Pour over the cider, let it bubble up, then add the cleaned mussels, discarding any that do not close when you tap them. Cover tightly with a lid and turn the heat to medium. Cook for 2 minutes, or until the shells have opened. Lift the mussels out with a slotted spoon and divide between 2 warm bowls (discarding any that remain closed). Cover the bowls to keep the mussels warm.

Turn up the heat and allow the cider to bubble away dramatically for 5 minutes, or until the liquid has reduced by one-third. Pour in the cream, stir and season with black pepper. Leave to bubble for another minute, then taste the sauce and, in the unlikely event of it needing salt, add a very little. Pour the sauce over the mussels and serve immediately, with crusty bread and a spoon for the cider sauce.

If you prefer your mussels cooked the classic French way, just swap the cider for white wine and you've got it. Easy as that!

Vietnamese PRAWNS & LEMONGRASS

The minuscule amount of preparation needed for this dish is worth every second as it is so quick to cook. This is fast food at its best and most authentic. Fat juicy prawns with a heady lemongrass sauce – truly too good to be believed, and made in less time and money than it would take to call it in from a takeaway, to boot. Quite possibly the easiest yet most impressive recipe in this book!

Heat the oil in a wok until it is smoking, then throw in the onion, spring onions and prawns. Stir-fry for 2 minutes, or until the prawns start to curl up and get a bit of colour on them.

Add the lemon juice, fish sauce, chilli powder, sugar, stock, lime leaves, shallots and lemongrass and bring to the boil for 1 minute. That's it! Serve with steamed rice and Oriental greens.

Serves 2
Preparation time 10 minutes
Cooking time 5 minutes

1 tablespoon groundnut oil
1 small onion, cut into slivers
2 spring onions, cut into 2.5cm pieces
12 large prawns, shelled and deveined
  (see p107)
the juice of 4 lemons
4 tablespoons Thai fish sauce
½ teaspoon chilli powder
2 teaspoons brown sugar
4 tablespoons chicken stock
2 lime leaves, thinly sliced
2 shallots, finely chopped
1 lemongrass stalk, finely chopped

Pan-fried SCALLOPS *with* CHORIZO, APPLES & MASHED POTATOES

Scallops and mash are a great pairing and make for fantastic comfort food. Now, mix in a bit of chorizo, with its incredible orange oil, and some apple, and you have comfort and gastro in the same bite.

Serves 4
Preparation time 10 minutes
Cooking time 10 minutes

3 tablespoons olive oil
16 hand-dived scallops, with or without roes
1 tablespoon butter
1 teaspoon sea salt
Creamy mashed potato (see page 74)
    made with double cream
2 Cox's or Braeburn apples, cut into
    small cubes
3 fresh chorizo sausages (I love the ones
    from Brindisa in Borough Market),
    cut into small cubes

Heat 1 tablespoon of oil in a pan until it starts to shimmer. Lay the scallops in a circle round the pan. Add the butter and let it foam up. Cook the scallops for about 1 minute on each side, or until crisp and golden.

Divide the hot mashed potato between 4 bowls. Remove the scallops from the pan and pop 4 into each bowl of mash.

To the same pan, add the remaining 2 tablespoons of oil, the apples and chorizo and stir-fry over a high heat for 2–3 minutes or until golden. Divide the chorizo and apples between the bowls of scallops and mash, and pour over the oil from the pan before serving.

WHY NOT TRY?

This recipe is also delicious if you use black pudding instead of chorizo.

Crispy-skin salmon
WITH WASABI SOBA NOODLES

This is an interpretation of one of my best friend Abbey's dishes, and I love it! It holds fond memories of me, Abbey and Julie munching away at it over a glass of wine while having a good old girly catch-up. It is a really tasty dish that you can throw together very quickly: the heady wasabi and creamy mayonnaise make a terrific dressing for the aromatic and bitey soba noodles and the crunchy veggies add texture. Abbey and I had a catering company for a few years and we used to serve this dish on Chinese soup spoons as canapés.

Serves 4
Preparation time 10 minutes
Cooking time 15 minutes

250g soba noodles (if you can find black ones, they'll look beautiful)
6 tablespoons soy sauce
4 tablespoons mirin (sweet rice wine)
a 3cm piece of fresh root ginger, peeled and grated
1 teaspoon sugar
4 salmon steaks, skin on
4 tablespoons mayonnaise
1 teaspoon wasabi
50g sugar-snap peas, sliced on the diagonal
½ red pepper, seeded and cut into matchsticks
1 medium carrot, peeled and cut into matchsticks
1 spring onion, cut into matchsticks
3 tablespoons groundnut oil
1 tablespoon sesame seeds

Cook the noodles according to the packet instructions. Meanwhile, mix the soy sauce, mirin, grated ginger and sugar in a bowl. Soak the salmon steaks in this marinade for 5 minutes, or longer if you want, although it's not really necessary here.

To make the noodle sauce, mix the mayo and wasabi together in a mixing bowl. Add the cooked warm noodles, along with all the veggies, and mix thoroughly. Divide between 4 plates.

Take the salmon out of the marinade and wipe off any excess. Reserve the rest of the marinade. Pan-fry the salmon, skin side down, in the oil for 6 minutes or until the skin has turned really golden and crisp, being careful not to cook it too quickly otherwise the sugar in the marinade will burn. Turn the salmon over and finish cooking it on the other side for a couple of minutes or until golden. Remove the salmon from the pan with a fish slice and drain on kitchen paper. Pour away the oil, then add the reserved marinade to the pan and leave it to bubble away until slightly syrupy.

Lay a piece of salmon on each plate, drizzle with a little of the marinade and sprinkle over some sesame seeds.

Chicken is always a favourite, especially as an everyday meal. I don't think a week goes by when I don't have a whole chicken and a few chicken thighs in the fridge. Roasting a whole chicken has to be one of the easiest things you can do, and it doesn't have to stop at a classic English roast with the trimmings. It's a totally normal occurrence for me to roast a chicken midweek, serve it with a baked potato, then use the rest of the bird to make a mean risotto or a super salad.

Tons of my foody memories as a child come from munching chicken. I remember being a kid and scrambling to get to my place at the table when the Sunday roast came along, or running round the garden on a hot summer's day eating crispy grilled chicken with the juices dripping down my arm, or that comforting feeling on a winter's day that comes from a good slow-cooked chicken casserole where the meat is melting off the bones.

In this chapter I have come up with recipes that I hope will both evoke those same memories, and also inspire you to move away from run-of-the-mill cooking.

★ ☆ Tips & Tricks ☆ ★

The average chicken that you buy from a supermarket is mass-produced, meaning the producer finds ways to make these birds grow quicker and in vast quantities. The result is horrific. Birds that are so cramped in their environment begin to weigh so much that their legs can break under them. They end up living in their own faeces for the last few weeks of their poor lives and are pumped full of antibiotics and hormones (which in turn filter out into our bloodstreams when we eat them). This is animal cruelty of the highest order, and by buying these products, however cheap, we are condoning the practice.

FACTORY-FARMED OR FREE-RANGE?

Free-range birds have a whole lot more space. The birds are allowed to develop at their natural rate and have to endure only a small percentage of the medication the factory-farmed birds get. You can see by their condition that they are much happier birds. For the sake of a few pounds it is so worth eating this way, not only because you're doing your bit for chickenkind, but also because the flavour is miles better.

WHAT CUT FOR WHAT?

* **A whole chicken:** Can be roasted, poached or cut into pieces for casseroling.

* **Chicken thighs/chicken legs:** Can be roasted, grilled, pan-fried or casseroled.

* **Chicken breast:** Grilled, pan-fried, poached or quick-cooked – do not slow-cook unless you want to crucify it.

PAN-FRYING & SAUTÉING

* Heat the frying pan until fairly hot. Add the oil, then place the chicken gently into the pan. Turn the heat down to a low medium – this will ensure you get a good colour on your meat, but that it also stays moist and cooks slowly on the inside.

* Always start frying poultry skin side down, so that the skin becomes really nice and crisp, remembering that you will need to cook the skin side for a little longer than the other side.

* Don't cover the pan with a lid while you are browning poultry or the moisture created will prevent it from browning properly.

* The second you cover your pan with a lid the skin will lose its crispness.

* To get the best colour, make sure the meat has quite a bit of space in the pan. This may mean you have to cook it in batches.

* Breasts need to be just cooked through in order for them to retain their moisture, but thighs will benefit from slightly slower, longer cooking.

ROASTING

☆ ☆

Chicken and turkey must be completely cooked through to prevent the risk of food poisoning, while duck, goose or game can be, and in most cases are better, served slightly pink.

✳ If stuffing the bird, account for the weight of the raw stuffing when working out cooking times.

✳ Chicken and turkey can dry out during cooking, so make sure you rub them with fat before you cook them. We cover birds in streaky bacon not just for flavour, but because it's a great way of basting the bird with fat during the cooking process.

✳ Fatty birds like duck need to be raised off the roasting tray to collect the fat, so sit them on a wire rack while cooking.

✳ To check that chicken or turkey is cooked through, poke a metal skewer into the leg and pull it out. If clear juices run out of the hole, it is cooked; alternatively, carve into the thigh with a small knife and see if it's cooked. Remember that thigh meat – especially in turkey – is much darker than breast meat.

ROASTING TIMES

BIRD	TEMPERATURE IN °C	COOKING TIME PER KG
Chicken	200	35–45 mins
Duck	190	45 mins
Goose	180	55 mins
Turkey	200	35 mins

STUFFING WHOLE BIRDS

There is a lot of controversy about stuffing birds. Do you put the stuffing in the cavity, or must it go under the skin? Is stuffing a bird risky, and should you avoid it altogether and bake the stuffing separately in balls or a loaf tin? Well, the answer has to be do whatever you feel comfortable with; just make sure the stuffing is piping hot when you serve it, or it may not be cooked properly.

I have always stuffed my birds in the cavity, as did my mother and as did hers, and none of us have ever had any trouble. I choose this technique because when the chicken cooks and rests, the juices ooze into the stuffing, which really benefits from this extra moisture and flavour.

The usual advice given is that if you want to be cautious, stuff the bird under the skin, and that those who are really nervous shouldn't stuff the bird and instead should cook the stuffing separately. All ways are fine, but there is one rule: whichever way you choose to do it, you must account for the stuffing in the weight of the bird when working out your cooking times, so weigh the stuffing separately before you stuff the bird.

A really good STUFFING

Makes enough to stuff a chicken; to stuff a turkey, double the quantities

Preparation time 10 minutes
Cooking time 15 minutes, plus the cooking time of the bird

1 tablespoon olive oil
200g good-quality smoked streaky bacon, finely chopped
1 onion, peeled and finely chopped
3 garlic cloves, peeled and finely chopped
a few sprigs of fresh thyme, leaves picked
450g sausagemeat
85g fresh white breadcrumbs
a small bunch of fresh parsley, chopped
zest of 1 unwaxed lemon
sea salt and freshly ground black pepper

Heat the oil in a frying pan. Add the bacon and fry for 5 minutes until it starts to turn slightly golden. Add the onion and fry over a lowish heat for 8 minutes, or until it has begun to soften. For the last minute of cooking, add the garlic and thyme.

Remove from the heat and add to a mixing bowl with the sausagemeat, breadcrumbs, parsley, lemon zest and a decent sprinkling of salt and pepper. Roll up your sleeves and get squelching it together, giving it a good mix to ensure everything is combined. Keep in the fridge until you are ready to use it.

WHY NOT TRY?

Sage and onion: Add another onion at the beginning of cooking, then replace the parsley with 5–6 sprigs of finely chopped sage.

Apricot and pistachio: Add 100g of chopped dried apricots and 200g of pistachio nuts to the stuffing mixture.

Apple and raisin: Add 1 peeled and grated cooking apple and 85g of sultanas.

Cranberry and walnut: Add 100g of dried cranberries and 85g of chopped walnuts to the stuffing mixture.

It is also unusual to stuff any bird other than a chicken or turkey under the skin as the skin tends to be either too thick or too thin, so if you want to stuff a goose or duck, for example, go for the cavity or cook the stuffing separately.

STUFFING THE CARCASS

Tip the bird so the cavity is facing upwards and wide open. Take fistfuls of the stuffing and push it into the cavity. Fill the bird up then round the stuffing off at the end, making sure you don't overstuff it because a little of the stuffing will be pushed out as it cooks.

STUFFING UNDER THE SKIN

From the neck end of the bird, carefully slide your hands under the skin to detach it from the meat – this is surprisingly easy and you can even detach the skin from the leg meat if you're careful. This is a great technique if you're going to line the bird with butter to add moisture while cooking. If you want to put stuffing under the skin, spread it evenly, smoothing it out as you go to create a really thin layer (around 5–8 mm). It will make the bird appear quite odd while whole, but it looks impressive when you carve the breast meat into slices.

COOKING STUFFING SEPARATELY

Either shape your stuffing into balls, or press it into a buttered loaf tin and carve it into slices (like a terrine) when cooked. You can also line the loaf tin with streaky bacon or wrap each ball in bacon to keep it moist while cooking.

My Mum's CHORIZO, PEPPER & RICE STUFFING FOR CHICKEN

Easter time in our household was always heralded by my mum's rice-stuffed roast chicken. She uses smoked bacon in place of chorizo, but I like it spicy, and the orange hue of the chorizo makes the dish so vibrant it perks up a whole lot. While the chicken cooks and rests, it oozes its juices into the rice, making it doubly delicious. The fab thing about this stuffing is that it doubles up as a side dish, so you can either serve it as a stuffing or have a spoonful of the fragrant rice with some crisp green salad.

Preparation time 15 minutes
Cooking time 20 minutes
Cooling time 30 minutes

1 tablespoon olive oil
2 fresh chorizo sausages, chopped
1 onion, finely chopped
3 garlic cloves, finely chopped
2 roasted red peppers, from a jar or the deli counter, chopped
a few sprigs of fresh thyme, leaves picked
½ teaspoon smoked paprika
200g cooked rice (use whatever rice you like – white, brown, wild, whatever takes your fancy)
a small bunch of flat-leaf parsley, chopped
sea salt and freshly ground black pepper

Heat the oil in a frying pan and throw in the chorizo. Sauté it over a lowish heat for a minute or two, then throw in the onions. Cook the onions and chorizo slowly for 8 minutes, or until the onions have softened and the chorizo is starting to char. The onions will be bright orange because of all of the paprika juices from the chorizo. Add the garlic in the last minute of cooking the onions.

Tip in the red peppers, thyme and paprika and sauté over a low heat for a minute. Add the rice and parsley and toss everything together. Leave to cool for 30 minutes and you're ready to get stuffing.

✩ MARVELLOUS MARINADES ✩

Marinades really are marvellous. It's just a matter of bunging a few ingredients into a food processor or blender, giving them a bit of a whiz, then massaging the marinade into the chicken and leaving it for a good few hours. All it takes is a little thought and you can turn a bog standard piece of chicken into a piece of scrumptiousness.

I'm not going to dictate what cut of chicken you use or how to cook it, that's up to you. All these marinades will work as well on a whole chicken as they will on slivers of meat on kebab sticks.

Bangkok CHICKEN MARINADE

Serves 4

3 tablespoons groundnut oil
4 large garlic cloves, peeled and roughly chopped
2 large shallots, peeled and roughly chopped
3 red chillies, roughly chopped
3cm piece of fresh root ginger, peeled and roughly chopped
1 tablespoon tomato purée
1 tablespoon Thai fish sauce
1 tablespoon soy sauce
1 teaspoon golden caster sugar or palm sugar
a bunch of fresh mint
a bunch of fresh coriander
15g roasted unsalted peanuts, chopped

Place all the ingredients in a food processor and blitz until smooth. Coat the chicken and leave to marinate for at least 2 hours but preferably overnight.

Malaysian SATAY MARINADE

Serves 4

2 garlic cloves, chopped
a bunch of fresh coriander
1 stem of lemongrass, roughly chopped
1 teaspoon curry powder
2 teaspoons ground turmeric
1 teaspoon brown sugar
½ teaspoon sea salt
½ teaspoon ground pepper (white if you have it)
250ml coconut milk
2 tablespoons soy sauce
1 tablespoon groundnut oil

Place all the ingredients in a food processor and blitz until smooth. Coat the chicken and leave to marinate for at least 2 hours but preferably overnight.

Fiery JERK MARINADE

Serves 4

2 tablespoons English mustard
2 tablespoons red wine vinegar
zest and juice of 2 limes
4 tablespoons runny honey
3 habanero (Scotch bonnet) chillies, deseeded and chopped
6 spring onions, roughly chopped
5 garlic cloves, chopped
a few sprigs of fresh thyme
a few sprigs of fresh oregano
½ teaspoon sea salt

Place all the ingredients in a food processor and blitz until smooth. Coat the chicken and leave to marinate for at least 2 hours but preferably overnight.

Peri peri MARINADE

Serves 4

juice of 2 limes
juice of 2 lemons
1 teaspoon paprika
1 teaspoon angostura bitters (if you have any lying around)
1 teaspoon Tabasco
1 chipotle chilli, soaked for 2 hours in boiling water, then stalk removed
2 garlic cloves
1 red chilli
2 tablespoons honey

Place all the ingredients in a food processor and blitz until smooth. Coat the chicken and leave to marinate for at least 2 hours but preferably overnight.

A spankingly GOOD CHICKEN KEBAB MARINADE

Serves 4

4 garlic cloves, chopped
1 red or green chilli, finely chopped
zest and juice of 1 unwaxed lemon
1 teaspoon smoked paprika
a few sprigs of fresh oregano
½ teaspoon sea salt
½ teaspoon freshly ground black pepper
4 tablespoons olive oil

Bash all the ingredients up using a pestle and mortar if you have one, otherwise just mix together in a bowl. Coat the chicken and leave to marinate for at least 2 hours but preferably overnight.

(SLIGHTLY BETTER FOR YOU) *Southern* FRIED CHICKEN (& GRAVY)

I'm about to make a confession that no foody should. I have a weakness for takeaway Southern fried chicken. Almost every time I walk past one of those horrible takeaway joints my friends have to rugby-tackle me away from them. The smell of frying chicken is up there with freshly baked bread or brewed coffee for me. The problem with takeaway places is that you can't guarantee the quality of the chicken, it's full of chemicals and tends to be fried in oil that's been used over and over again. But re-creating it yourself with free-range chicken breast, coated in a spiced flour and shallow-fried in olive oil possibly makes this kinda good for you . . . well at least that's what I'm going to tell myself. Serve it the soul food way with mashed potatoes and coleslaw.

Serves 4
Preparation time 10 minutes
Cooking time 15 minutes

300ml buttermilk or plain yoghurt
a splash of milk
3–4 skinless and boneless free-range chicken breasts, each cut into 6 or 7 pieces
100g plain flour
¾ teaspoon sea salt
½ teaspoon ground white pepper
½ teaspoon freshly ground black pepper
½ teaspoon celery salt
½ teaspoon cayenne pepper
½ teaspoon paprika (hot if you want it spicy)
150ml olive oil (you may need a spot more by the time you cook the last batch)
400ml chicken stock

Purple coleslaw: To make a delicious low-fat coleslaw, finely slice ½ a red onion and mix well in a bowl with 100g thinly sliced red cabbage, 100g thinly sliced white cabbage, ½ a bulb of fennel, thinly sliced, 6 thinly sliced radishes, 100g of Greek yoghurt, 1½ tablespoons of red wine vinegar, ½ teaspoon of celery seeds, ½ teaspoon of fennel seeds, salt and pepper.

Mix together the buttermilk or yoghurt and milk in a bowl, then add the chicken and stir to coat. Some people believe you should marinate the chicken in this mixture for 20–30 minutes to tenderise it, and if you have time, why not?

In a second bowl mix together the flour, seasoning and spices. Heat the oil in a deep frying pan or sauté pan until it's shimmering.

Toss the chicken in the spiced flour, making sure it gets a really good thick coating. Add the chicken pieces to the oil in batches and fry for 4–5 minutes on each side, or until crisp, golden and cooked through. With a slotted spoon remove the chicken and drain on kitchen paper. Repeat with the rest of the chicken. Don't throw away the flour.

To make the gravy, pour the oil into a heatproof container, leaving about 1 tablespoonful plus all the crispy bits in the bottom of the pan, as they will add to the flavour. Stir in 1 tablespoon of the leftover spiced flour and let it cook for a minute. Slowly stir in the chicken stock until the gravy is smooth. Bring to the boil, then simmer until thickened and reduced. American chicken gravy is much thicker than ours, somewhere between a gravy and white sauce, I'd say. There is quite a lot of seasoning in the flour, so you will not need any salt.

Coq au vin with HERBY DUMPLINGS

Classically, the French would not dream of serving coq au vin with dumplings, but as I am not French I don't care! When the dumplings rise and soak up all the winey cooking liquid, they create such a taste and texture sensation that I very much doubt you will be worrying about their authenticity.

Serves 4
Preparation time 20 minutes
Cooking time 1 hour 30 minutes

2 tablespoons olive oil
8 free-range chicken thighs, boned, skinned and halved
sea salt and freshly ground black pepper
16 baby button mushrooms
4 rashers of smoked streaky bacon, cut into lardons
2 banana shallots, peeled and finely sliced
1 large carrot, peeled and finely diced
3 garlic cloves, peeled and chopped
1 tablespoon plain white flour
1 tablespoon tomato purée
600ml red wine
300ml chicken stock
1 bouquet garni (bay leaves, fresh thyme and fresh parsley, tied into a bundle)

For the dumplings
100g self-raising flour
½ teaspoon salt
1½ teaspoons olive oil
a small handful of fresh parsley, chopped
3 teaspoons snipped fresh chives
60ml semi-skimmed milk

Preheat the oven to 180°C/gas 4. Heat 1 tablespoon of oil in a large, heavy-based, lidded casserole. Season the chicken thighs with salt and pepper. Brown in the pan in two batches for 4 minutes on each side, then set aside. Throw in the mushrooms and cook in the remaining oil for 5 minutes, or until golden. (If the pan appears dry, add a little boiling water and scrape the bottom of the pan to pick up any chickeny residue.) Set the mushrooms aside with the chicken.

Add the remaining tablespoon of oil to the pan. Add the bacon and fry over a high heat for 2 minutes. Reduce the heat and add the shallots and carrot. Cover them with the lid and sweat over a low heat for 10 minutes, adding the garlic to the pan for the last minute. Add the plain flour and tomato purée and stir, coating the vegetables for 1 minute.

Gradually pour in the wine, stirring as you go to emulsify the sauce. Add the stock, chicken, mushrooms and bouquet garni and stir through. Place in the oven and cook, covered, for 1 hour, stirring halfway through the cooking time.

To make the dumplings, mix all the ingredients together and shape into 8 small balls. For the last 20 minutes of the casserole cooking time, add the dumplings and cover with the lid. They will double in size during cooking. Remove the lid for the last 5 minutes' cooking time so that they become golden on top.

Moroccan CHICKEN COUSCOUS

There is a difference between a tagine and a couscous. A tagine is a thicker stew, cooked in the funny-shaped clay pot they call a tagine. Whereas a proper couscous is served with a Moroccan spiced, brothy stew that's dotted with big chunks of root veg and chickpeas. You serve a proper couscous drenched in this stew and with harissa, but how much depends on how brave you are. Harissa gets quite hot. Try a few varieties out. I love rose harissa – it's both fiery hot and aromatic.

Heat the oil in a large heavy-bottomed pan. Add the chicken pieces and cook until brown all over. You may need to do this in batches. Remove the chicken with a slotted spoon and set aside.

Add the onions to the pan and cook for 5 minutes, or until they have softened and started to go golden. Make sure you really scrape away at the chickeny residue at the bottom of the pan. Add the garlic and chillies for the last minute of cooking.

Add the salt, spices, bay leaves and thyme sprigs and cook for a further minute. Pour over the stock, then return the chicken to the pan along with the turnips, carrots and courgettes. Cook for 40 minutes – the chicken should be melting off the bones. Add the chickpeas for the last 10 minutes of cooking.

Meanwhile, put the couscous into a large mixing bowl and add the salt and enough boiling water to cover it by 8mm. Cover with clingfilm and leave to soak for 10 minutes, then remove the film and fluff up with a fork. Dress with the olive oil and lemon juice and stir in the chopped coriander.

Serve the chicken stew on top of the couscous, with a good dollop of harissa alongside.

Serves 4
Preparation time 20 minutes
Cooking time 1 hour

3 tablespoons vegetable oil
1 whole chicken, cut into 8 pieces, or
 8 chicken thighs, skinned
2 large onions, cut into eighths
4 garlic cloves, chopped
2 green chillies, finely chopped
1 teaspoon sea salt
½ teaspoon freshly ground black pepper
½ teaspoon cayenne pepper
1 teaspoon cumin
1 teaspoon paprika
2 bay leaves
a few sprigs of fresh thyme
1½ pints chicken stock (fresh if you have it)
2 turnips, peeled and quartered
4 carrots, peeled and cut into 3
2 large courgettes, halved lengthways and
 each half cut into 3
1 x 400g tin of chickpeas, drained and rinsed
harissa to serve

For the couscous
300g couscous
a pinch of salt
2 tablespoons extra virgin olive oil
juice of ½ lemon
a small bunch of fresh coriander, finely
 chopped

Sticky BARBECUE CHICKEN WINGS WITH BLUE CHEESE DRESSING & *celery*

Chicken wings are an archetypal example of a cheap meat packed full of flavour that cooks really well. And there is no denying that nibbling on chicken wings and getting spicy, sticky barbecue sauce all over your fingers and face is one of life's great pleasures. The cool blue cheese and soured cream dip takes the edge off the heat in the sauce. Use it to dip the chicken wings in, or the celery, or, as I like to do, both!

Makes 40 pieces
Preparation time 10 minutes
Cooking time 1 hour

20 free-range chicken wings, cut into winglets by cutting through each of the joints, keeping the 2 meaty pieces and discarding the wing tips to make 40 pieces
2 tablespoons olive oil
sea salt and freshly ground black pepper

For the barbecue sauce
150ml tomato ketchup
120ml cider vinegar
4 tablespoons soft dark brown sugar
2 tablespoons hot sauce (I love chipotle Tabasco, as it is so smoky and works brilliantly in barbecue sauce)
1 teaspoon ground cumin
1 teaspoon smoked paprika
½ teaspoon salt
black pepper

For the blue cheese dressing
100g blue cheese, preferably Gorgonzola
200ml soured cream
a squeeze of lemon juice
sea salt and freshly ground black pepper

4 celery stalks, cleaned, each one cut into 4 small stalks

Preheat the oven to 220°C/gas 7. Lay the chicken pieces on a large baking sheet, drizzle with olive oil and sprinkle with salt and pepper. Pop them into the oven and let them roast for 20 minutes, then reduce the temperature to 180°C/gas 4 and cook for a further 40 minutes.

To make the barbecue sauce, put all the ingredients together in a pan and let it bubble away for 3–5 minutes to thicken up a little. Taste and add more seasoning if necessary.

Thirty minutes before the end of the chicken wings' cooking time, take them out of the oven and coat them in half the barbecue sauce. Then, when fully cooked, toss them in the rest of the sauce so that they become sticky. They are just as delicious served straight from the oven as they are cold.

While the chicken is in the oven, it's the perfect time to get on with the blue cheese dressing. Mash together the cheese, soured cream, lemon juice and salt and pepper until combined (a few lumps are nice, though).

Serve the wings with the celery stalks and the blue cheese dressing.

Griddled WHITE-PEPPER-CRUSTED GUINEA FOWL WITH GREEN APPLE SALAD

We don't eat a lot of guinea fowl in this country and I have no idea why. It's cheap, it has more flavour than chicken yet is not too 'gamey', it's simple to cook and it's becoming really easy to get hold of. This simple Thai marinade is crammed with authentic flavour. The green apple salad is my variation on the classic som tam or Thai green mango salad. I couldn't find green mangoes one day and the crisp, tart green apple was an obvious alternative – and jolly nice it is too.

Lay the guinea fowl on a chopping board and cut it into quarters. Put them into a bowl. In a food processor, whiz together the white pepper, salt, lemongrass, ginger, garlic and oil until it becomes a paste. Cover the guinea fowl with the paste and leave to marinate for at least 2 hours, or overnight if you have time.

Preheat the oven to 180°C/gas 4 and heat a griddle pan until almost smoking. Lay the guinea fowl on the griddle and cook for 4 minutes on each side, or until golden and slightly charred. Place on a baking sheet and roast in the oven for 15 minutes, then remove and leave to rest for 5 minutes.

To make the dressing, whiz together the garlic, chilli and sugar to make a rough paste. Add the fish sauce and lime juice, and season to taste.

For the salad, fry the shallots in the oil for around 5 minutes or until crisp and golden brown. Remove with a slotted spoon and drain on kitchen paper. Toss the apples in a bowl with the lime juice and add the tomatoes and dressing. Spoon on to plates and top with the peanuts, crisp shallots and coriander.

Slice the guinea fowl into 1cm-thick slices. Place on the plates with the salad and serve.

Serves 2
Preparation time 25 minutes
Marinating time 2 hours minimum
Cooking time 30 minutes

1 guinea fowl, boned (get your butcher to do this for you)
1 teaspoon white pepper
1 teaspoon sea salt
2 stalks lemongrass, roughly chopped (woody outer leaves discarded)
a 3cm piece of fresh root ginger, peeled and roughly chopped
3 garlic cloves, peeled
2 tablespoons groundnut or vegetable oil

For the dressing
1 garlic clove, peeled and finely chopped
1 red chilli, seeded and finely chopped
1 teaspoon golden caster sugar
1 tablespoon Thai fish sauce
juice of 2 limes
sea salt and freshly ground black pepper

For the salad
3 shallots, peeled and finely sliced
1 tablespoon vegetable oil
4 sharp green apples, such as Granny Smith's, cored and cut into thin strips
1 tablespoon lime juice
6 cherry tomatoes, cut into quarters
2 tablespoons dry roasted peanuts, crushed
a handful of fresh coriander leaves, chopped

Pan-fried DUCK BREAST *with* FLATBREAD, SOURED CREAM & SALAD

We're so used to seeing duck served alongside fruit or Asian style, mainly because the acidity of fruit cuts through the richness of the duck. But they do a pretty mean duck dish in Eastern Europe using cream and cucumber. I've made my own bread in the dish, but you could always use white pitta and fry it in the duck fat released through the cooking at the end. Not great for the ticker, but delicious all the same.

Serves 4
Preparation time 15 minutes
Cooking time 20 minutes (not including bread-making)

1 portion of white bread dough (see page 215), or 4 pitta breads
olive oil
4 duck breasts, skin on
sea salt and freshly ground black pepper

For the salad
1 cucumber, peeled, seeded and thinly sliced into half-moons
¼ teaspoon salt
280ml soured cream
1 small pack of fresh dill, finely chopped
smoked paprika

SEX IT UP!

To really impress, serve this with pomegranate molasses and sprinkled with pomegranate seeds.

If making your own bread, preheat the oven to 170°C/gas 3. Cut the risen bread dough into 4 pieces and roll each piece into a 1cm-thick, round disc. Cover each disc with oiled clingfilm and leave to prove for 10 minutes. Heat a griddle pan until almost smoking. Using a pastry brush, grease each disc of dough with olive oil. One by one lay the dough discs on the griddle and grill for 3 minutes on each side, or until the bread has risen and is golden. Leave the bread in the oven to keep warm while you get on with the duck.

Heat a frying pan until very hot and lay the duck breasts in the pan, without oil. Reduce the temperature to medium, and pan-fry for 8 minutes or until the fat has drained away into the pan and the skin has turned golden and crisp. Turn the duck breasts over and cook on the other side for 4 minutes to give a perfect pink colour. Remove the duck breasts from the pan, reserving the pan juices, and leave to rest, uncovered so that the skin stays crisp, for 5 minutes. Slice the duck breasts into thin slices.

To make the salad, simply mix together the cucumber and salt and leave to drain for 10 minutes in a sieve so the excess water begins to come out of the cucumber. Mix the drained cucumber with the soured cream, dill and a pinch of paprika and season with pepper.

Serve each duck breast on a disc of grilled bread, with some salad alongside. Pour over the juices from the duck, then drizzle with olive oil and sprinkle with a spot more paprika.

It is constantly being said that our health is affected (for the worse) by eating too much meat. On the other hand, there is ever more sophisticated and intensive rearing that is designed to encourage us to eat more. Unfortunately, the result of this type of farming is an obvious decline in the welfare and quality of our meat.

The only way to guarantee better meat and a better qualiy of life for these creatures would be to cut down on the amount of meat we consume. This would eventually end intensive rearing, a process that does not allow the animal to grow or mature correctly. The flavour of our Highland beef, Welsh mountain lamb, and pork from animals with freedom to roam in fields or orchards is impossible to beat.

Meat would, of course, become more expensive, though that too would help manage the levels of consumption. But just think of the compensation of eating a big fat juicy steak with its remarkable quality and flavour. And frankly, meat should be expensive – you can't put a cheap price on the life of an animal, especially if its welfare is at stake.

So next time you go to reach for a packet of orange meat from the supermarket it might be worth thinking of the consequences of what you're doing. Speak to your local butcher, find out where your meat comes from and how it has been treated both in its life and after it. After all, if we are going to eat meat we should be getting the best out of it and doing it with a clean conscience.

TIPS & TRICKS

Meat should be a rich, dark red colour. We are used to seeing orange meat in the supermarket, but this will have little flavour – a deeper, richer colour is a clear indication that the meat has been well hung and that the animal has had a good diet and lifestyle. The longer the animal is dry hung, the darker it can go; I have eaten some incredible meat that was virtually black when raw!

HOW TO BUY MEAT

* The texture of steak should be very close and quite dry. If you can distinguish the grains and it feels wet, the meat is not at its best.

* Look for a good 'marbling' of fat throughout the meat, which means it should have lots of veins of fat distributed through it. The rule with meat generally is that fat means flavour.

* The fat should be a pale, creamy colour and not too yellowy; nor should it have excessive fat around the outside.

* Fresh meat smells clean.

* Freezing meat is perfectly acceptable, but when it defrosts it loses liquid which will change the quality – so always use fresh when you can.

ROASTING

* You can brown meat before roasting by searing it over a high heat in a little oil in a roasting pan.

* Alternatively, get your oven really hot for the first 20 minutes of cooking, and then reduce it for the latter part. A good browning temperature is 220°C/gas 7 and a good roasting temperature is 180°C/gas 4.

* Make sure the oven has been preheated.

* Rest the meat, covered with foil, for at least 20 minutes before carving, so that the juices can return to the surface. This also means you have time to make the gravy and cook your veggies.

FRYING, GRILLING OR GRIDDLING STEAK

* Make sure you have a really hot pan before you start. You don't want it smoking the house out, but it should be a little smoky. This will ensure you colour the meat well.

* Don't use too much oil or your meat won't brown properly. For great colour, use either a mix of butter and oil or just butter.

* Make sure you season the meat with lots of salt and pepper just before you cook it. You will be surprised at how much flavour it adds to the meat.

* Don't overcrowd your pan or the meat will boil rather than brown. If this means cooking your steaks one at a time, so be it!

* If the pan is hot enough to begin with, leave it to cook for exactly the same amount of time on both sides.

* Leave steak to rest for 5 minutes before you serve it, then pour all the lovely juices over it or add them to your sauce.

★ ☆ BEEF ☆ ★

The best beef is aged, which means it has been hung for at least 14 days. The longer meat is hung, the stronger the flavour, as hanging dries it out and tenderises it at the same time. For really strong flavour, look out for dry-aged meat. Dry ageing is when the meat is left to age in a dry atmosphere so it dries out a bit, thus condensing the flavour. Unless you're buying from the meat counter or it is clearly indicated on the packaging, you will rarely find dry-aged, well-hung beef in a supermarket, so look locally for a good butcher.

COMMON CUTS

★ **Steak**: Cooking a steak properly is really easy, but so many people get it wrong. Think about when you go to restaurants and order steak. They normally use a searingly hot griddle, which is the key to a good steak. I'm not suggesting you have an indoor barbecue fitted in your house, but what this tells you is that a steak needs to be cooked on something really hot.

So, say you have a 2.5cm-thick piece of steak. Heat a griddle or frying pan until it is smoking hot. Season the meat with plenty of sea salt and freshly ground black pepper, pop a splash of oil, a bit of butter or a mixture of both into a pan, then grill or pan-fry it for 2 minutes on each side. Do not move it about the pan, let the meat stick to the pan and caramelise on the outside before whipping it over and doing the same on the other side. What you're looking for is a really charred dark outside and a nicely pink middle. As with all meat, you must leave it to rest for a good 5 minutes before serving.

For me it's all about béarnaise sauce (page 242) or a good butter (page 146), some fat chips and not much else.

There are many different cuts of steak and for some people it comes down to preference, while I feel they all serve a purpose. So I'm just going to try to describe them here and leave it to you to choose what you think is best...

★ **Fillet steak:** The leanest (and most expensive) of the steaks. Normally thick cut, it has delicate flavour because it has very little fat, and fat is flavour. These steaks are so tender they require minimal chewing. I think it's best used for things you might want to sear – it is the cut you choose for Chateaubriand and for beef Wellington.

★ **Sirloin steak:** Taken from the middle, back end of the loin of the animal. A sirloin steak has a fair bit of flavour and is quite an easy and firm cut to cook with. It has more bite than a rib-eye, but is not the firmest of the steaks. Also know as the New York strip or entrecote.

★ **Rib-eye steak:** At the centre of the rib of beef you find the rib-eye. A complex piece of meat that has quite a lot of fat, but as it does not do much work it is still a super tender cut. It is by far the tastiest piece of meat you can eat, in my view. A côte de boeuf is a really thick-cut rib-eye steak for two and a real treat at that! My favourite steak.

★ **Rump steak:** Once upon a time rump steak was a fairly cheap cut; nowadays, as it has an abundance of flavour, it is getting a spot pricier, although still not touching its counterparts in the sirloin, rib-eye or fillet regions. I use rump to make steak sandwiches with, and it's great for barbecuing as it holds its shape well.

★ **T-bone steak:** When I think of Desperate Dan I think of the humungous chop that he used to eat – the T-bone. This cut is simply a piece of sirloin and a piece of fillet joined together with its natural T-shaped bone. A great cut of meat, as you get a piece of really tender meat and a sturdy, flavoursome piece of sirloin. Fantastic to whip out if you want some 'wow' factor.

𝓑𝓾𝓽𝓽𝓮𝓻𝓼 FOR STEAKS

I said before that butter is one of the best things to have with steak and it's so easy, just mashing a bunch of ingredients together and chilling them in the fridge before adding a slice on your cooked steak.

GARLIC & HERB BUTTER
Makes about 100g

100g unsalted butter, at room temperature
1–2 small garlic cloves, peeled and finely grated
50g chopped mixed herbs (I would use parsley, tarragon and thyme)
sea salt and freshly ground black pepper

BLUE CHEESE & TOASTED PECAN BUTTER
Makes about 300g

100g unsalted butter, at room temperature
170g blue cheese (I love to use Stilton for this)
50g toasted pecans, chopped
1 small garlic clove, peeled and finely grated
1 tablespoon finely chopped fresh chives
sea salt and freshly ground black pepper

THAI CHILLI, LIME, CORIANDER & MINT BUTTER
Makes about 100g

100g unsalted butter, at room temperature
juice and zest of 1 lime
1–2 small garlic cloves, peeled and finely grated
1 red chilli, finely chopped
25g chopped fresh coriander
25g chopped fresh mint
sea salt and freshly ground black pepper

Place the butter in a mixing bowl and mash together with the rest of the ingredients for your chosen butter. Put between 2 sheets of clingfilm or greaseproof paper and roll into a tight sausage shape. Store in the fridge for 2 hours before using.

ROASTING CUTS

* **The rib:** The prime roasting joint.

* **The sirloin:** Delicious and easy to carve.

* **Topside:** The cheapest and most used roasting cut; I feel it's always a bit tough.

BEEF ROASTING TIMETABLE

	TEMPERATURE IN °C	COOKING TIME PER KG
Browning	220	20 mins
Rare	180	30 mins
Medium Rare	180	35 mins
Medium	180	40 mins
Well Done	180	50 mins

STEWING CUTS

* **Steak**: Shin: As the legs do so much work and are naturally sinewy, a slow-cooked shin will be gelatinous and melt-in-the-mouth.

* **Chuck:** Most of the stewing meat we buy is chuck, and it's great because it doesn't need the really long slow cooking of shin. But then it doesn't quite have its flavour either. Really good mince comes from chuck, and if you're going to ask for it yourself then get a 20% fat version.

* **Oxtail:** The tail of the cow, cut into pieces at each joint. When slow-cooked, the meat on this baby is toothsuckingly good. As it's so close to the bone it has tons of flavour, and it oozes loads of gelatine when cooked, giving a sticky sauce.

While on the subject of beef, a couple of un-beefy recipes that I know will keep the beefeaters happy…

Yorkshire PUDDING

Makes 12 small Yorkshires or 1 giant one

There is a secret to Yorkshire pudding and it's simply this: even quantities of each of the main ingredients. The way I do it is by cracking the eggs into a glass, then measuring how high they come up the glass. Pour the eggs into a bowl then fill the glass to the exact same level with first flour then milk; mix together. This is a fail-safe way of making Yorkshire puds, and means you don't need to bother getting the weighing scales out. However, if you feel a bit unsure here is a recipe. The other part of the secret is piping hot oil and a hot oven. There needs to be a sizzle when you pour in the batter.

Preparation time 5 minutes
Resting time
Cooking time 30–35 minutes

3 free-range eggs
85g plain flour
150ml milk
½ teaspoon salt
freshly ground black pepper
3–4 tablespoons oil or fat (you can use vegetable, olive or corn oil or beef dripping)

Heat the oven to 200°C/gas 6. Place the eggs, flour and milk in a bowl and whisk until smooth and combined. You can do this in a food processor or mixer if you like. Add the salt and season with pepper, then leave in the fridge for between 10 minutes and 1 hour to rest.

Fill either a 12-hole Yorkshire pudding tin or a medium ovenproof dish or frying pan with the oil or fat, and pop it into the oven to heat up for 10 minutes.

Pour the mixture into the holes in the tin or into the ovenproof dish or pan, and place in the oven for 30 minutes. The puddings will rise massively and become firm on the outside but fluffy and spongy in the middle. Remove them from the tin, stand them on kitchen paper to drain and serve immediately.

Yorkshire puddings are superb with roast beef and sausages, but frankly they are essential with any Sunday roast.

Horseradish SAUCE

Makes 150ml

The horseradish is the most spectacular root. It puts ginger to shame when it comes to power and heat. You come across it more and more now, and not just in farmers' markets – even my local shop has started stocking it. If you are a fan of heat, make your horseradish sauce yourself – it is a whole heap more fierce and packs a punch that simply cannot be jarred! Not just for beef though – try it with smoked or oily fish, tomatoes or beetroot.

Preparation time 20 minutes

15g freshly grated horseradish
1 tablespoon white wine vinegar
a pinch of English mustard powder
½ teaspoon golden caster sugar
sea salt and freshly ground black pepper
150ml double cream, lightly whipped

Soak the horseradish in 2 tablespoons of boiling water until cool. Drain, and mix with all the other ingredients. Leave in the fridge to soften for at least 20 minutes.

★ ☆ PORK ☆ ★

PAN-FRYING OR GRILLING CUTS

✴ **Loin chops:** The chop from the loin.

✴ **Neck chops:** The chop that is cut from the neck. It has the most flavour of all the chops in my opinion.

✴ **Pork fillet:** Deliciously tender cut of pork that's great for everything from grilling to stir-fries.

ROASTING CUTS

✴ **Loin roast:** The typical roasting joint cut from the loin. It's an expensive cut but a real crowd-pleaser.

✴ **Shoulder of pork:** The most amazing meltingly tender cut of pork if cooked right, with long slow cooking. Frankly this cut produces the best crackling too.

✴ **Pork Belly:** This popular cut is notoriously cheap, and is scrumptious. Slow-cook it so the fat melts out of it, leaving the most toothsome meat.

Pork cooking times: Allow 20 minutes' browning time at 220°C/gas 7, then reduce the temperature to 190°C/gas 5 and cook for 25 minutes per 450g for a standard roast.

STEWING CUTS

✴ **Pork leg:** A yummy piece of meat that produces the most sensational stews.

✴ **Belly pork:** More common as a roasting cut, but do as the Asians do and use it for slow braises.

A mighty fine APPLE SAUCE
Makes 150g

Can you imagine roast pork without apple sauce.Nope, me neither, and as ever it's all too easy to go out and buy a jar. But, needless to say, it tastes a damn sight better when you make it yourself.

3 Bramley apples, peeled, cored and sliced
50g caster sugar
juice and zest of 1 unwaxed lemon
60g butter

Tip all the ingredients into a pan and cover with a lid. Place the pan on a low heat, stirring occasionally, for about 15 minutes, until the apples break down into a purée. Stir to knock out any lumps, and tip into a serving dish.

LAMB

PAN-FRYING OR GRILLING CUTS

✶ **Lamb chops:** Very versatile and easy to eke a meal out of.

✶ **Lamb fillet:** A premium cut of meat and expensive too. It is super tender, but I feel it lacks flavour.

✶ **Best end of neck:** Possibly the most expensive cut of lamb. Can be carved to make lamb cutlets or have the bones removed to give a really tender piece of meat that makes a mean medallion.

✶ **Leg of lamb:** A flavoursome cut of meat that works brilliantly cubed for kebabs and makes delicious, if slightly tough, steaks.

ROASTING CUTS

✶ **Leg of lamb:** One of the best roasting cuts. Delicious both fast or slow roasted.

✶ **Shoulder of lamb:** Under-used and has loads of flavour. Superb slow-roasted until falling off the bone.

Lamb cooking times: allow 20 minutes' browning time at 220°C/gas 7, then reduce the temperature to 180°C/gas 4 and cook for 20 minutes per 450g for medium (or pink) lamb. Add another 20 minutes at the end of cooking for well-done lamb.

GOOD STEWING CUTS

✶ **Leg of lamb:** Cut into cubes it makes a super cut for stewing. What most of us know and love.

✶ **Neck fillet:** My favourite stewing cut, so sinewy that when cooked properly it falls apart and has loads of flavour.

✶ **Lamb shanks:** Ah, the sumptuous lamb shank. Quite swanky to show off to your friends with when cooking for them, cheap and flavoursome.

Mint SAUCE

Roast lamb cries out for mint sauce and as with any fresh herb sauce, for example pesto and salsa verde, you will never get the impact unless you use the freshest of fresh herbs. Especially where mint is concerned. You do need to give it a bit of time to soak, but the result outshines its jarred counterparts.

Makes 150ml

a large bunch of fresh mint
a pinch of salt
50ml boiling water
50ml white wine vinegar
2 tablespoons caster sugar

Strip off the mint leaves and place them in a blender with a pinch of salt. Add the boiling water and whiz, then transfer to a jug and leave to cool.

Mix together the vinegar and sugar and pour over the mint purée. Have a taste and see if it needs some more vinegar or sugar.

Proper BEEF STEW

Sometimes the simplest things are the most delicious, and on a cold winter's night a steaming plate of beef stew and mashed potatoes really is good, hearty food at its best.

Serves 4
Preparation time 20 minutes
Cooking time 2½ hours

2 tablespoons olive oil
500g stewing beef, cut into 4cm chunks
   (if buying from a butcher, ask for beef shin)
1 onion, peeled and chopped
2 carrots, peeled and chopped
½ swede, peeled and chopped
2 stalks of celery, chopped
2 leeks, chopped
1 teaspoon tomato purée
1 tablespoon plain flour
570ml beef stock
2 sprigs of fresh rosemary, leaves picked
a few sprigs of fresh thyme, leaves picked
2 bay leaves
sea salt and freshly ground black pepper

Preheat the oven to 170°C/gas 3. Heat 1 tablespoon of oil in a medium, heavy-based casserole pan. Season the meat, then brown in batches. Remove each batch of meat with a slotted spoon and set aside on a plate.

Add the rest of the oil to the pan, along with the veggies and cook over a low heat for 10 minutes or until softened and slightly caramelised. Add the tomato purée and flour to the pan and cook for a minute.

Pour in the stock. Return the meat to the pan and add the herbs, then cover the pan with a lid and place in the oven for 2 hours, or until the meat is falling apart and the sauce has thickened slightly. Season to taste before serving piping hot with mash.

Taleggio & SAGE-STUFFED PORK CHOPS WITH ROASTED apples

Pork chops, sage and apple – you don't get much more British than that – so I thought I'd throw some Taleggio cheese into the mix. The cheesy melting middle is a scrummy surprise, and the whole thing is drenched in sage butter for some Anglo-Italian magic.

Preheat the oven to 200°C/gas 6. Place the apple halves on a baking sheet and dab each one evenly with 1 teaspoon of butter. Pop a couple of sage leaves on top, and sprinkle with the sugar. Bake the apples in the oven for 20 minutes – you want them to be soft in the middle and crisp and caramelised on the outside.

Meanwhile, slice a pocket into each pork chop along the edge that doesn't have the bone along it. (You need to slice fairly deep into the chop, about three-quarters of the way through.) Stuff each chop with a slice of Taleggio and a couple more sage leaves. Season the chops with lots of salt and pepper.

Heat 25g of butter in a frying pan with the rest of the sage. When it's really hot (but not so hot that it begins to burn), add the chops and fry for 2 minutes on each side. For the last few minutes of cooking the chops, add the rest of the butter to the pan. Transfer the chops to the same roasting tray as the apples, pouring the sage butter over them, and roast in the oven for a further 5 minutes.

When you remove the apples and chops from the oven the chops will be oozing with melting cheese. Leave them to rest for 5 minutes, then serve each chop with 2 apple halves and some of the buttery juices.

Serves 4
Preparation time 15 minutes
Cooking time 25 minutes

4 Braeburn apples, halved and cored
50g butter, plus 8 teaspoons
a small handful of fresh sage leaves
1 teaspoon golden caster sugar
4 pork loin chops (they look beautiful French-trimmed, so ask your butcher to do this for you)
150g Taleggio cheese, cut into 4 long, thin slices
sea salt and freshly ground black pepper

WHY NOT TRY? Swap the apples for 4 pears and you've got another great dish.

Parma ham & SAGE-WRAPPED *veal* WITH TOMATO SPAGHETTI

My sisters and I were brought up on veal Milanese (breaded veal with spaghetti and tomato sauce), and I wanted to bring the dish into the twenty-first century. For this recipe I have combined my two favourite Italian veal dishes, saltimbocca and Milanese, and have made the spaghetti sauce sweeter and fresher by using tinned cherry tomatoes (a fab store-cupboard ingredient). I came up with something which, after feeding my two sisters, will go down in Erskine history. This one's for you, Munds and Bubs!

Serves 4
Preparation time 15 minutes
Cooking time 30 minutes

20 fresh sage leaves
100g fresh white bread, crusts removed
4 x 150g veal escalopes (go for British rose veal if you can find it – better flavour, happier cows – or, if you still feel funny about veal, bash out some pork chops or chicken breasts)
4 slices of Parma ham
1 large free-range egg, lightly beaten
100g plain flour
sea salt and freshly ground black pepper
100ml olive oil

For the cherry tomato and basil spaghetti
1 tablespoon olive oil
1 small onion, peeled and finely chopped
3 garlic cloves, peeled and finely chopped
2 x 400g tins of cherry tomatoes
1 tablespoon tomato purée
1 teaspoon golden caster sugar
a splash of sherry vinegar or red wine vinegar
a small bunch of fresh basil
sea salt and freshly ground black pepper
350g spaghetti
lemon wedges and Parmesan cheese, to serve

Put the sage leaves and bread into a food processor and whiz until you have fragrant breadcrumbs. Lay the veal escalopes on a chopping board and cover each one with a couple of sheets of clingfilm. Using a meat tenderiser or a rolling pin, bash each escalope until it is about 2-3mm thick.

Wrap each escalope with a couple of slices of Parma ham (you may need to use some of the egg to stick these down). Season the flour with salt and pepper, then put the flour, egg and bread-crumbs into separate bowls. Dip each escalope into the flour, then coat with the beaten egg and finally with breadcrumbs. Put the escalopes into the fridge to chill while you make the spaghetti sauce.

Heat the 1 tablespoon of oil in a small pan. Throw in the onion and cook over a low heat for around 8 minutes, or until softened. For the last minute of cooking, add the garlic. Add the tinned tomatoes to the pan along with the purée, sugar, vinegar and the basil, torn into pieces. Season with salt and pepper and leave to bubble away for 20 minutes. Halfway through, get the spaghetti cooking in plenty of boiling, salted water.

Once the spaghetti is on, heat the 100ml of oil in a frying pan. Lay the breaded escalopes into the oil carefully (if they are very large you may need to cook them one at a time). Fry the escalopes for 3 minutes on each side, depending on how thick they are, until the breadcrumbs are golden brown. Drain them on kitchen paper. Drain the spaghetti and mix with the cherry tomato sauce. Serve the spaghetti with the veal, some lemon wedges and a shaving of Parmesan cheese if you like.

Milk-roasted pork with
CINNAMON, ORANGE & BAY

It may sound unusual, but milk tenderises pork while it's cooking. At the same time, the cinnamon, orange, fennel seeds and bay release their aromas and the juices run out of the pork. These flavours merge into the most sensational sauce: a peasant dish fit for a king! Be careful not to overcook pork: people think it should be eaten well done, but it can be amazing when it's just over medium, making it nice and moist.

Serves 6
Preparation time 20 minutes
Cooking time 2 hour 15 minutes

1kg pork loin (it looks beautiful French-trimmed, so ask your butcher to do this for you)
1 tablespoon ground coriander
1 tablespoon fennel seeds
sea salt and freshly ground black pepper
2 tablespoons olive oil
570ml full-fat milk (or mix 1 tablespoon double cream into 555ml semi-skimmed milk)
1 stick cinnamon
zest of 1 orange
3 bay leaves
1 teaspoon plain flour
400ml chicken stock
1 tablespoon double cream (optional)

Preheat the oven to 180°C/gas 4. If your butcher has not already done it, with a sharp knife slash the crackling fat. Mix together the coriander, fennel seeds, 1 teaspoon salt and ½ teaspoon pepper and rub this into the flesh and the fat of the pork. On the hob, heat the oil in the smallest roasting tray the pork will fit into. Lay the meat fat side down and fry the fat first – it may spit like crazy, so be careful. Brown the rest of the pork all over, then remove it from the heat. Pour the milk into the roasting tray, add the cinnamon, orange zest and bay leaves, then pop the tray into the oven. Roast for 1 hour 30 minutes, basting the pork with the milk every 25 minutes. The milk will reduce during the cooking. It looks pretty ugly, but don't worry because when you make your sauce it will all come back together.

When it is time to remove the pork from the oven, you should be able to poke a skewer into it and, when you take it out, the juices should run clear. The crackling should be lovely and crisp, but if it isn't quite there yet, slice it off the meat and put it back into the oven for 10 minutes.

Leave the pork to rest for 20 minutes. Then remove it from the tray and leave to rest for a further 10 minutes. Pour the milky porky residue and aromatics (cinnamon, orange zest and bay) into a small pan. Whisk in the flour and heat until it begins to bubble. Add the stock bit by bit, then leave it to bubble away on a low heat for 2–3 minutes, or until it has begun to thicken. Sieve the sauce to get the aromatics and any larger lumps out; the sauce will still have fine lumps and if this really bothers you, stir in a tablespoon of double cream, although I don't think it needs it. Season the sauce. You should get hits of all the flavours, and the milk will add natural sweetness. Serve the pork cut between the bones like chops, with a drizzle of sauce.

$\mathscr{Basic}$ ROASTED FIVE-SPICE PORK BELLY

Anyone who has eaten pork belly knows that there is not much out there that matches its glorious meltiness. The perfect pork always has crisp crackling and meat so tender it falls apart under your fork. Most pork belly recipes call for the pork to be rubbed with crushed cumin seeds and roasted, but pork belly is also a classic Asian ingredient and adores spices. So here I have rubbed it with Chinese five-spice powder, which is a mixture of cinnamon, coriander, star anise, Sichuan pepper, cloves and the pork classic, fennel seeds. This basic roasting recipe cooks the pork slowly until it falls apart and is a great dish to have in your repertoire! See the following two recipes for my suggestions for what to serve it with.

Preheat the oven to 230°C/gas 8. Rub the pork with olive oil and then rub the salt, five-spice and pepper all over the skin and the meat. Place the pork on a rack in a roasting tray and bake for 20 minutes.

Reduce the oven temperature to 180°C/gas 4 and bake for a further 1 hour 30 minutes. Leave to rest for 15 minutes before carving. If the crackling isn't crisp enough, slice it off in one piece and return it to the oven on a high heat for 15 minutes while you rest the pork under foil.

Serves 8
Preparation time 10 minutes
Cooking time 2 hours

a 1.3kg piece of belly pork, with an even
  thickness, rind scored (ask your butcher to
  do this, as thinly as possible)
1 tablespoon olive oil
1 teaspoon sea salt
1 tablespoon Chinese five-spice powder
  (or, if you are just having a regular roast,
  1 tablespoon fennel seeds)
½ teaspoon freshly ground black pepper

Roasted PORK BELLY with APPLE, PLUM & STAR ANISE SAUCE

We all know that pork and apple sauce is a winner, but with pork belly infused with Chinese five-spice, I wanted to see if I could come up with an Asian-style apple sauce. With the addition of plums, star anise and soy, I do believe I've nailed it.

Serves 4
Preparation time 10 minutes
Cooking time 2 hours 20 minutes

1 x basic roasted five-spice pork belly (see page 155)
2 Bramley apples, peeled and chopped
2 red plums, stoned and chopped
1 tablespoon soy sauce
1 star anise
1 tablespoon golden caster sugar
1 tablespoon plain flour
1 glass white wine
200ml chicken stock
300g purple sprouting broccoli

Prepare the roasted pork belly. While it is roasting, place the apples, plums, soy sauce, star anise and caster sugar in a pan over a low heat and cook gently for about 15 minutes. Leave to cool.

While the meat is resting, you can make a light gravy by tipping out the excess fat, bar about a tablespoonful, from the roasting tray. Add the flour to the tray and, while scraping away at the residue on the bottom, allow to cook for a minute. Slowly tip in the wine while continuing to scrape the pan. You may want to switch to a whisk in order to avoid getting lumps in your gravy! Whisk in the stock and bring to the boil for about 5 minutes, or until slightly syrupy. Strain into a gravy boat.

Steam or boil the purple sprouting broccoli for 3 minutes. To serve, slice the pork into 3cm-thick slices and serve with the broccoli, some gravy and a big dollop of the Asian apple, plum and star anise sauce.

WHY NOT TRY?

This goes really well with creamy mashed potato (see page 74)

Roasted PORK BELLY *with* BLACK RICE VINEGAR & ASIAN GREENS

The sweet and salty vinegar cuts though the sticky fatty pork, creating balanced yin and yang. This is perfect as a meal in itself and, what's more, it's the best way to make two meals out of one with any pork belly you may have left over from your Sunday roast. Just fry the cubes of pork in a little oil until they have crisped up and you're good to go.

Prepare the roasted pork belly. While it is resting, mix together the vinegar, soy sauce, chilli oil, and spring onions to make the dipping sauce, and divide between 4 small bowls.

Steam the mixed Asian greens for 4 minutes, or until they are cooked through but still have some bite.

When the pork has rested, chop it into 2.5cm cubes. Pour the pork juices into the dipping sauce.

To serve, place some greens in each of 4 fresh bowls and top with a few cubes of pork.

Serves 4
Preparation time 10 minutes
Cooking time 2 hours 5 minutes

1 x basic roasted five-spice pork belly
  (see page 155)

For the dipping sauce
3 tablespoons black rice vinegar (if you can't
  find it, use rice wine vinegar)
6 tablespoons Kikkoman soy sauce
1 tablespoon chilli oil
6 spring onions, thinly sliced

400g Asian greens (pak choi, choi sum and
  tender-stem broccoli)

Serve this with steamed rice for a more complete meal.

Lamb chops with
GREEN PEPPERCORN *sauce*

But peppercorn sauce is for beef, I hear you say! Traditionally yes, but one day I was craving peppercorn sauce but only had lamb chops at home, which is how I discovered that it is great with lamb as well. Somehow this usually rich and indulgent sauce becomes lighter and more fragrant. Give it a go – I know you'll be swayed.

Serves 4
Preparation time 5 minutes
Cooking time 20 minutes

8 lamb chops
1 teaspoon olive oil
sea salt and freshly ground black pepper

For the sauce
240ml brandy
3 tablespoons green peppercorns in brine,
   drained, half of them chopped
480ml lamb or beef stock
240ml double cream
a large knob of cold butter
a small bunch of fresh parsley, chopped
green salad, to serve

Rub the chops with the olive oil and season with salt and pepper. Heat a large griddle pan over a high heat and, when the pan is hot, add the chops and cook for 2 minutes on each side for medium rare (or until cooked to your liking). Set the chops aside to keep warm while you make the sauce.

Put the brandy and peppercorns into a small sauté pan and bring to the boil. Let the brandy bubble away for 3 minutes, or until syrupy. Add the stock to the pan and continue to simmer for about 10 minutes, until reduced by half. Stir in the cream and boil for another 3 minutes, then whisk in the butter and parsley. The sauce should be thick and glossy.

Place a couple of chops on each plate, spoon over the sauce and serve immediately with a green salad.

WHY NOT TRY?

As you'd expect, this green peppercorn sauce is also excellent with steak.

Spiced MANGO-ROASTED *ham*

Most butchers nowadays will tell you it's unnecessary to soak a ham, so don't be put off making this if you don't have enough time to soak the ham overnight.

Put the ham into the biggest pot you can find, preferably a deep, wide stockpot into which it will fit easily. Pour over the mango juice and top up with water to cover the ham. Add the onions, carrots, leeks, spices and bay leaves. Slowly bring the liquid to the boil – you will see a scum forming on the surface. Using a large spoon, carefully remove the scum as it appears and repeat until the surface appears clear.

Once the liquid is bubbling, turn down the heat to a fast simmer and allow it to blip away for 3 hours, topping up the water level regularly with cold water and removing scum from the surface every time you do so.

Once the ham is cooked (it will start to pull away from the bone), remove it from the pan very carefully so as not to tear any of the meat. You may find it easier to let the ham cool a little in the cooking liquor, then allow it to drain and cool in a colander for 10 minutes.

Place the ham in a large roasting tin. Very carefully, slice the skin to reveal the thick layer of white fat, then score the fat crossways in both directions so there are loads of little diamond shapes all over it.

Preheat the oven to 180°C/gas 4. In a pan, melt together all the glaze ingredients, except for the cloves. Rub the glaze all over the ham and push a clove into the corner of each diamond shape. This not only makes the ham look really beautiful, but also releases the most amazing aroma as it cooks. Place the ham in the oven and roast for 40 minutes, until sticky and caramelised. Leave it to rest for an hour if you want to eat it warm, or let it cool completely. Personally I think ham is best served with mashed or boiled new potatoes, salad and chutneys and pickles.

Serves 10–15
Preparation time 12 hours (if soaking the ham)
Cooking time 4 hours
Resting time 1 hour

1 smoked, boned and rolled gammon ham, soaked overnight in loads of cold water (change the water a few times)
1 litre mango juice
2 medium onions, peeled and quartered
2 carrots, peeled and halved
2 leeks (whites only), halved lengthways
6 whole cloves
2 star anise
8 allspice berries
10 black peppercorns
2 bay leaves
mashed or boiled new potatoes, salad and chutneys and pickles, to serve

For the glaze
4 tablespoons mango chutney
2 tablespoons butter
1 teaspoon mixed spice
1 teaspoon smoked paprika
50 whole cloves

Breaded lamb cutlets
WITH SALSA VERDE

I remember having breaded lamb cutlets for the first time in a tapas bar in Spain. Lamb is light enough to carry the crumbs without them becoming really rich. The salsa verde is to die for, with a herby, citrusy tang, the anchovies just adding enough seasoning to carry the dish and give it backbone. Just a dollop wakes up the whole dish and packs a mega punch exactly where you want it!

Serves 4
Preparation time 15 minutes
Cooking time 10 minutes

2 racks of lamb, or 3–4 cutlets per person
  (either middle neck, which is cheaper, and
  has more flavour but only 5 bones, or best
  end of neck, which is more delicate and
  more expensive, with 8 bones)
100g plain flour
sea salt and freshly ground black pepper
1 large free-range egg, lightly beaten
200g fresh breadcrumbs
a small handful of fresh mint, finely chopped
1 tablespoon capers, finely chopped
100ml olive oil

For the salsa verde
1 or 2 garlic cloves, peeled
a small handful of capers
a small handful of pickled gherkins or
  cornichons
6 anchovy fillets
2 large handfuls of fresh flat-leaf parsley
a bunch of fresh basil leaves
a handful of fresh mint leaves
1 tablespoon Dijon mustard
3 tablespoons sherry vinegar
juice of ½ lemon
150ml best-quality olive oil
sea salt and freshly ground black pepper

Cut the lamb into cutlets and lay them on a board. Place a double sheet of clingfilm over the top of each one and bash them to flatten them a bit, although you want them to still be about 5mm thick, rather than really thin like an escalope.

Place the flour (which you should season with lots of salt and pepper), egg and breadcrumbs in separate bowls. Add the chopped mint and capers to the breadcrumbs and mix thoroughly.

Dip each cutlet first into the flour, then into the egg (coating them well, as the egg will act like glue), and finally into the breadcrumbs. Set the breaded cutlets aside for a few minutes while you make the salsa verde.

Place all the salsa verde ingredients into a food processor and blitz. (Some purists claim you should hand-chop all the ingredients, and if you can be bothered, go for it – frankly, though, it makes little difference and saves a whole heap of mess and time doing it with a machine!)

Heat the 100ml of oil in a frying pan. Add the breaded cutlets and cook for 2 minutes on each side, or until the crumb has turned golden brown; you want the cutlets to be pink inside, so be careful not to overcook them. Serve with a dollop of salsa verde on the side of each plate.

PUDDINGS & ICE CREAM

10

My love affair with puddings started when I was first asked to help my mother with the Sunday roast. She would start off with two jobs: one was peeling the vegetables and the second was helping with the pudding. I remember even at that age feeling a sense of achievement at turning all these store-cupboard ingredients (another wonder of puddings) into a tantalising pudding, and I remember the torture of watching whatever creative tart she had made cooling on the windowsill.

Like most people I am nostalgic about puddings and love how they evoke memories – so I therefore feel the best of the bunch are the type your mother would have made.

However, saying that, you can look in most books and find out how to make a crumble or apple pie, so I want to take these classics into the twenty-first century. Look at sticky toffee pudding. There's not much you can do to that to make it better … or is there? By adding banana and a bit more of the toffee element we now have a sticky banoffee pudding. It's even better – try it for yourself and you'll see. And the Baileys chocolate croissant butter pudding is in a league of its own.

With the world constantly telling us to count calories and watch what we eat, I see a vast amount of value in giving yourself a bit of what you fancy every now and then. After all – the 'everything in moderation' philosophy is a good one to live by, and deprivation only leads to gorging. So tuck in, that's what I say.

TIPS & TRICKS

BAKED PUDDINGS

✳ Always preheat the oven for a baked pudding.

✳ The oven temperature will be quite high, between 180°C and 200°C.

✳ Always weigh out your ingredients before you start.

✳ Always butter your dish.

✳ If you want to make individual portions, these recipes should each split into 6 individual ones.

✳ If the pudding requires beating, this will be much easier with an electric whisk.

✳ If a pudding has baking powder, a raising agent or whipped egg white in it you will need to get it into the oven pronto, but if it doesn't, for example a custard-based pud like the Baileys chocolate croissant butter pudding, you can make it in advance and set it aside until you want to bake it.

PUDS

MERINGUES

✳ Always line your baking sheets with baking parchment or silicone.

✳ Use a Pyrex or copper bowl: for some reason, plastic ones just don't do it.

✳ Make sure all your equipment is very clean – even the smallest trace of oil can spoil your meringue.

✳ Make sure there is no trace of egg yolk in your whites. Remember, egg yolks are full of fat and your meringue will not work.

✳ The older the egg whites, the better they whisk. This does not mean that fresh eggs won't work, though! Just whisk them with a tiny pinch of salt, as this will break up the egg 'threads'.

✳ Use room-temperature eggs.

✳ When you whisk you are adding air to the meringue, so start slowly and build up speed towards the end.

✳ It is possible to over-whisk egg whites, so don't go too mad. If you feel the eggs starting to get loose again, it means that you have started to whisk the air out. Annoyingly, it's a fine line, so just remember to stop once the eggs feel really stiff.

✳ You can add ¼ teaspoon of cream of tartar to stabilise the foam, and sometimes a splash of white wine vinegar is added to help keep them gooey.

Basic MERINGUE RECIPE

Makes 10 meringues

A good meringue is crisp, ever so slightly flaky on the outside and marshmallowy, but not foamy, in the middle. While this recipe is for making individual meringues, you can also use it for the top of lemon meringue pie or baked Alaska.

Preparation time 10 minutes
Cooking time 1 hour
Cooling time 1 hour

4 large free-range egg whites
200g golden caster sugar

Preheat the oven to 140°C/gas 1. Whisk the egg whites with an electric mixer or beater until firm and beginning to hold their peaks. Then gradually whisk in the sugar, 1 tablespoon at a time, patiently whipping until you have a stiff, shiny meringue.

Line 2 baking sheets with greaseproof paper. Spoon (or pipe if you're feeling a bit retro) dollops of the meringue mixture, about 2 dessertspoonfuls per meringue – on to the sheets and spread out to make 8–10cm diameter blobs. Shape the tops into swirls and peaks so they look gorgeous. Make sure you leave some space between the meringues because they will puff up a little while they cook.

Cook for 45 minutes to 1 hour, then turn off the oven and leave them to cool inside. When ready, they should be dry on the outside and still feel a little soft on the inside. Once out of the oven, leave them until completely cold before you try to move them, as they are fragile and may shatter.

WHY NOT TRY?

Meringues with cream and rhubarb, strawberry and Pimm's compote
Place 6 chopped rhubarb stalks, 1 tablespoon of sugar and 4 tablespoons of Pimm's in a oven preheated to 180°C/gas 4 and bake for 10 minutes. Add 400g strawberries and cook for a further 5 minutes. Carefully mix together, then leave to cool (if the syrup seems too thin, you can thicken it by boiling until it reduces). Serve on top of your meringues with whipped double cream.

Passion fruit Eton mess
Crush 4 meringues and mix with 300ml of whipped double cream, then swirl through a few tablespoons of passion fruit curd (see page 252) and the pulp of 1 or 2 passion fruits. Serve in bowls or glasses.

★ ☆ PANCAKES ☆ ★

★ Don't over-beat your batter otherwise the pancakes will be tough and chewy.

★ Keep your batter quite cold. Cold batter tends to set better and make a crisper pancake.

★ Make sure your batter has time to rest in the fridge. A good 30 minutes should do it.

★ Always have everything you need ready to go, as pancakes cook really quickly.

★ It is sod's law that your first pancake is a disaster even the best chefs get this, so don't let it put you off.

Pancakes

I know they say that a bad workman blames his tools, but I truly believe that I didn't start making great pancakes until I invested in a pancake pan. They have a low rim, which means you can slide a palette knife underneath with ease, so flipping becomes easy. Resting your batter is important too. It gives the flour time to expand and relax, which will give a nice light pancake.

Makes 8-10

Preparation time 5 minutes
Resting time 30 minutes
Cooking time 20 minutes

110g plain flour
a pinch of salt
a pinch of sugar
1 free-range egg
1 free-range egg yolk
285ml milk
2 tablespoons vegetable oil
* or melted butter*

Put the flour, salt and sugar into a mixing bowl. Gradually whisk in the egg, egg yolk and milk until smooth and combined. Cover with clingfilm and leave to rest in the fridge for 30 minutes.

Heat a pancake/crêpe pan to a medium heat. You must make sure the pan is fairly hot before spooning in the batter, otherwise you will get thick rubbery pancakes. Dip a piece of kitchen paper into the oil and wipe round the pan. Add 1 ladleful of batter into the pan and swirl it around, making sure it coats the bottom. Pour any excess batter back into the bowl. Fry the pancake for 30 seconds to 1 minute, until the pancake is nicely golden on its base, then carefully flip it over and finish cooking it for a further 30 seconds. This side will have small brown blisters on it. Slide the pancake on to a plate and repeat with the rest of the batter.

WHY NOT TRY?

If you're feeling naughty, serve your pancakes with some Cointreau cream. Simply whip 150ml of double cream with 2 tablespoons of Cointreau and 1 teaspoon of icing sugar.

Ice Cream & Sorbet

No matter what anyone says, in my opinion you cannot get the best out of your ice cream by home churning (mixing every few hours while the ice cream freezes). Ice cream machines give a much better result, and are a good investment if you want to get into ice cream making.

✳ Make sure you do not overcook the custard base, as it will scramble.

✳ Sieve the custard to make sure it is really smooth.

✳ Churn the ice cream properly or you will find that it contains ice crystals when you serve it.

✳ If ice cream does not freeze properly, there is either too much sugar in it, it's not been frozen for long enough or you have added too much booze.

✳ If adding alcohol to sorbet, be careful – remember, some alcohols don't freeze.

It is important that you have the right consistency of sugar syrup when making sorbets, and they are surprisingly less syrupy than you'd expect.

Sticky BANOFFEE PUDDING

This is my boyfriend Dean's recipe. While he is a fantastic cook, he is so lazy he never cooks for me, except for this. And my God, does it make up for it! The banana is terrific with the toffeeish dates and keeps the pudding really moist.

Serves 6
Preparation time 15 minutes
Cooking time 40 minutes

250g dates, stoned and chopped
250ml hot black tea, made with 1 teabag
1 teaspoon bicarbonate of soda
85g softened unsalted butter, plus extra butter
  for greasing
175g caster sugar
2 large free-range eggs, beaten
175g self-raising flour, sieved
3 bananas, roughly mashed
1 teaspoon ground mixed spice
vanilla ice cream, or clotted cream, to serve

For the sauce
100g light muscovado sugar
100g unsalted butter
150ml double cream

Preheat the oven to 180°C/gas 4 and butter a 22cm baking dish. Place the dates in a small pan and cover with the hot tea. Bring to the boil and cook for 3–4 minutes, until the dates have softened, then stir in the bicarbonate of soda.

Cream together the butter and sugar until light and fluffy, then add the eggs, one at a time. Fold in the flour, banana, mixed spice and the date mixture and pour into the baking dish. Bake for 30–35 minutes, until the top is springy and a skewer comes out clean when inserted into the centre.

While the pudding is cooking, make the sauce. Put the muscovado sugar, butter and cream into a pan, place over a low heat and melt until the sugar has dissolved. Then whack the heat up and simmer for 3–4 minutes, or until the sauce is a light toffee colour.

Serve the pudding with the warm sauce and a big scoop of vanilla ice cream or clotted cream.

WHY NOT TRY?

Remove the bananas and you've got a classic sticky toffee pudding.

Baileys chocolate croissant
BUTTER PUDDING

I came across a similar recipe to this while working at *BBC Good Food*. It was a pivotal point in my pudding-making career, as I had never before tasted anything quite so amazing. I have made it my own (and even better) by adding even more booze to the custard and simply making it really gooey. Be warned: it is one of those puddings that has you believing that you can eat the whole lot.

Serves 6
Preparation time 20 minutes
Cooking time 20 minutes

50g golden caster sugar
1 large free-range egg
5 free-range egg yolks
300ml Baileys cream liqueur
400ml double cream
butter, for greasing
6–8 chocolate croissants, torn into pieces
70g light muscovado sugar

For the butterscotch sauce
100g light muscovado sugar
100g butter
150ml double cream

Preheat the oven to 200°C/gas 6. Whisk the caster sugar, whole egg and egg yolks together in a bowl. Put the Baileys and 400ml of double cream into a pan and bring to the boil. Whisk this in to the egg mixture, then leave until cooled slightly to make a custard.

Lightly grease a 30 x 20cm baking dish with butter. Place a layer of croissant pieces in the base and add a generous sprinkle of muscovado sugar and a little of the egg custard. Keep on layering croissants, sugar and custard in the same way, finishing off with a sprinkling of sugar. Let the pudding sit for 10 minutes so it soaks up all the custard, then bake for 18–20 minutes, until puffed up, golden and crisp (the muscovado sugar will give a tasty and sticky finish to the pudding).

While the pudding is baking, make the sauce. Place the sugar and butter in a pan and stir over a medium heat until melted. Pour in the cream and bring to the boil. Reduce the heat and simmer for 3–4 minutes, until dark and sticky. To serve, scoop out servings of the pudding and pour over a little of the warm butterscotch sauce.

Peach, RASPBERRY & ALMOND SLUMP

'What on earth is a slump?' I hear you asking. Well, it's somewhere between an upside-down cake and a clafoutis. An American invention, it's an easy pudding that can be whizzed together in just a few ticks.

Preheat the oven to 180°C/gas 4. In a food processor, whiz together the butter, sugar, flour, eggs, milk and vanilla extract until smooth. Lightly grease an oval 20 x 30cm baking dish or a deep 20cm cake tin. Mix together the peaches, raspberries, Amaretto and sugar and lay them in the base of the tin.

Dollop over the cake mix, then smooth it all over with the back of a spoon so that it covers the fruit. Make a little dip in the middle of the mixture to ensure it cooks evenly throughout. Scatter over the almonds.

Cook for 45 minutes, until the fruit is hot and the sponge is cooked through. Serve warm, with custard or vanilla ice cream.

Serves 6
Preparation time 10 minutes
Cooking time 45 minutes

100g softened butter, plus extra for greasing
100g caster sugar
100g self-raising flour
2 large free-range eggs
1 tablespoon milk
1 teaspoon vanilla extract
2 peaches, stoned and cut into 8 slices
250g raspberries
4 tablespoons Amaretto liqueur
1 tablespoon sugar
25g flaked almonds

WHY NOT TRY?

Instead of peaches and raspberries, make this with 3 Bramley apples and 250g of blackberries.

Lemon & PASSION FRUIT SELF-SAUCING *pudding*

My mum makes the most amazing pudding called lemon surprise tart, which is a crisp pastry tart with gooey lemon sponge in the centre. It is so calorific, though, that I wanted to see if I could make it a little kinder on the waistline. By ditching the crust, you end up with a self-saucing sponge pudding that leaves a wicked custardy curd at the bottom. With the addition of passion fruit, this makes a really light end to your meal and is great for Sunday lunch after a heavy roast.

Preheat the oven to 170°C/gas 3. Whiz the butter, sugar and lemon zest in a food processor until pale and creamy. Add the lemon juice, passion fruit juice, egg yolks, flour and milk, one ingredient at a time, until you have a smooth batter.

Whisk the egg whites until firm but not stiff and fold them into the batter.

Pour into a buttered baking dish and place in a baking tray. Half-fill the baking tray with hot water (to make a bain-marie). Put this in the oven and bake for 45–50 minutes, until the top is lightly browned and set and there is a sort of gooey curd below. Remove the dish from the tray and serve hot, with cream and raspberries.

Serves 4–6
Preparation time 20 minutes
Cooking time 50 minutes

50g butter, plus extra for greasing
150g caster sugar
juice and zest of 1 unwaxed lemon
120ml passion fruit juice (about 16 passion fruits)
3 large free-range eggs, separated
50g plain flour, sifted
250ml milk
cream and fresh raspberries, to serve

White chocolate
& HONEYCOMB CHEESECAKE

This is officially the cheesecake to beat all cheesecakes. I made this cake for one of my friends and dressed it with shards of white chocolate and blood-red and black roses. It looked (and tasted) tremendous.

Preheat the oven to 170°C/gas 3. Line the base of a 23cm springform cake tin with parchment paper. For the biscuit base, stir the melted butter into the biscuit crumbs and sugar until evenly mixed. Press the mixture into the base of the tin and bake for 10 minutes. Leave to cool while you prepare the filling.

Increase the oven temperature to 200°C/gas 6. In a food processor beat the cream cheese at medium low speed until creamy, then gradually add the sugar, flour and vanilla extract.

Whisk in the eggs and yolk, one at a time. Add the soured cream and the melted white chocolate and whisk to blend, but don't over-beat. The batter should be smooth, light and a little airy.

Pour into a mixing bowl and stir in the chopped Crunchie bars.

Brush the insides of the springform tin with melted butter and place it on a baking sheet. Pour in the filling and bake for 15 minutes, then reduce the oven temperature to 110°C/gas ¼ and bake for a further 25 minutes, or until the filling wobbles slightly when you gently shake the tin. When it has reached this point, turn off the oven and either open the oven door for a cheesecake that's creamy in the centre, or leave it closed if you prefer a drier texture. Either way, leave it to cool in the oven for 2 hours. The cheesecake may crack slightly on top as it cools.

Cover loosely with foil and refrigerate for at least 8 hours or overnight. When ready to serve, run a round-bladed knife around the inside of the tin to loosen any stuck edges. Unlock the side of the tin, slide the cheesecake on to a plate, and very carefully slide the parchment paper out from underneath before serving.

Makes 12 slices
Preparation time 15 minutes
Cooking time 3 hours
Chilling time 8 hours

85ml melted butter, plus extra for greasing
200g ginger biscuits, whizzed to fine crumbs
   in a food processor
1 tablespoon golden caster sugar

For the filling
3 x 300g packs of full-fat cream cheese
   (Philadelphia is good)
250g golden caster sugar
3 tablespoons plain flour
1 teaspoon vanilla extract
3 large free-range eggs
1 free-range egg yolk
284ml carton of soured cream
300g white chocolate, melted
3 Crunchie bars, trimmed of their chocolate
   and chopped into pieces

WHY NOT TRY?

Remove the chocolate and the Crunchie bars and you've got a great classic New York baked cheesecake.

Chocolate brownie
ICE CREAM

Until recently, if you'd asked me what ice cream flavour I would go for, I'd say chocolate! But having researched and researched chocolate ice cream recipes, I've struggled to find a great one. Some are too weak, some too strong, some too creamy, some not creamy enough. Here's my solution!

Preparation time 15 minutes
Cooking time 10 minutes
Cooling time 30 minutes
Churning and freezing time 3–5 hours,
  or preferably overnight

250ml milk
300ml double cream
150g plain chocolate (70% cocoa solids),
  finely chopped or grated
55g golden caster sugar
5 large free-range egg yolks
1 teaspoon vanilla extract
85g crumbled chocolate brownies (you could
  use the marbled chocolate brownies on
  page 195)

Heat the milk, cream and chocolate in a small non-stick pan until bubbles start to rise up the edges. In a separate bowl, whisk the sugar, egg yolks and vanilla extract together, then in a slow stream carefully pour in the hot milk, whisking continuously. Pour the custard back into the pan and, using a wooden spoon, scrape the bottom of the pan while cooking it gently for a minute or so or until it thickens enough to coat the back of the spoon. (Be really careful – the eggs can scramble quite easily, and if it starts to look grainy it has gone too far.)

Strain the custard into a bowl and leave it to cool, covered with clingfilm. This will take about 30 minutes, but you can speed the process up by placing the bowl of custard in an ice bath.

Set up your ice cream machine, pour the custard into it and leave to churn for 20 minutes. Add the brownies and churn for a further 25 minutes, or until smooth and frozen. Transfer the ice cream to a freezerproof container and freeze for at least 2 hours before eating.

WHY
NOT
TRY?

Chocolate ice cream: Omit the brownies from the recipe and you have a tremendous rich chocolate ice cream.

Butter caramel
& HONEYCOMB ICE CREAM

Wickedly decadent, this pudding has a grown-up bittersweet quality to it that little ones don't really appreciate yet adults flock to. But that doesn't mean we have to ignore our childish side: a pack or two of crushed Crunchie bars stirred through the ice cream before it has set in the freezer should do the trick, as the honeycomb in a Crunchie is both sticky and crunchy. Can you imagine?

Put the sugar into a dry frying pan and melt over a low heat until it starts to caramelise – you want it to be a nice mid-brown colour, not too light or too dark. Stir in the butter and 250ml of double cream, then leave to cool a little.

While the caramel is cooling, heat the milk and rest of the cream in a small non-stick pan until bubbles start to rise up the edges. In a separate bowl, whisk the egg yolks and vanilla extract together, then in a slow stream carefully pour in the hot milk, whisking continuously. Pour it back into the pan and, with a wooden spoon, scrape the bottom of the pan while cooking the custard gently for a minute or so, until it thickens enough to coat the back of the spoon. (Be really careful – the eggs can scramble quite easily, and if it starts to look grainy it has gone too far.)

Strain the custard into a bowl and leave it to cool, covered with clingfilm. This will take about 30 minutes, but you can speed the process up by placing the bowl of custard in an ice bath.

Whisk the cold custard into the caramel until combined. Set up your ice cream machine, pour the caramel custard into it and leave to churn for 20 minutes. Add the chopped Crunchie bars and churn for a further 25 minutes or until smooth and frozen. Transfer the ice cream to a freezerproof container and freeze for at least 2 hours before eating.

Serves 6
Preparation time 10 minutes
Cooking time 10 minutes
Cooling time 30 minutes
Churning and freezing time 3–5 hours,
*   or preferably overnight*

300g golden caster sugar
4 tablespoons salted butter
500ml double cream
250ml whole milk
5 large free-range egg yolks
1 teaspoon vanilla extract
2 Crunchie bars (or 2 x 37g packs of
   Maltesers), chopped

WHY NOT TRY?

Salted caramel ice cream: Instead of Crunchie bars, add ¾ teaspoon of Maldon sea salt halfway through churning.

Lemon & ELDERFLOWER SORBET

As a child I couldn't wait for pudding at an Italian restaurant, as this meant eating creamy lemon sorbet out of a carved-out lemon. Tacky as it sounds, I now find that concept incredibly retro and, therefore, incredibly cool! But how do we take the sorbet of sorbets into the twenty-first century? By mixing the lemon with elderflower for a refreshing sorbet that's both floral and sour.

Put the sugar and elderflower cordial into a pan with 750ml water. Heat gently until the sugar dissolves then stir in the lemon juice, zest and glucose syrup (if using). Bring to the boil for 2–3 minutes, then leave to cool for 30 minutes in an ice bath.

Set up your ice cream machine, pour in the liquid and churn until smooth and frozen. Transfer to a freezerproof container and freeze for 3–5 hours before eating.

Makes 750ml
Preparation time 10 minutes
Cooking time 10 minutes
Cooling time 30 minutes
Churning and freezing time 3–5 hours,
*   or preferably overnight*

400g golden caster sugar
100ml elderflower cordial
250ml lemon juice (6–8 lemons)
zest of 1 unwaxed lemon
3 tablespoons liquid glucose (optional)

Gin & PINK GRAPEFRUIT SORBET

I felt like an old lush even contemplating this recipe, but gin and grapefruit are exceptional together so I gave it a go and as expected, it's a winner! The bitter sourness of the grapefruit benefits from the shot of gin, which adds an aromatic cleanness to it. The taste of it makes me think of sunshine, lawns and croquet, the Queen Mum and all things English. Eat it as a sorbet or as a palate cleanser between courses.

Put the grapefruit juice, sugar and water into a pan. Heat gently until the sugar dissolves, then stir in the liquid glucose. Bring to the boil for 2–3 minutes. Leave to cool for 30 minutes in an ice bath. Finally add the gin.

Get your ice cream machine set up, pour the liquid into the machine, and churn the liquid until smooth and frozen. Transfer to a freezer container and freeze for 3–5 hours before eating.

Preparation time 10 minutes
Cooking time 10 minutes
Cooling time 30 minutes
Churning and freezing time 3–5 hours,
*   or preferably overnight*

juice of 7 pink grapefruits
270g golden caster sugar
450ml water
4 tablespoons liquid glucose
4 tablespoons gin (I love Plymouth gin)

There is something comforting about sinking your teeth into a pillowy sponge, getting buttery icing on the tip of your nose, crumbs falling into your lap. One of the only foods we actually sit back and savour, it's no wonder cakes are an institution in this country.

Most cakes consist of five different components: fat, sugar, eggs, flour and raising agents. We expect most of our tea cakes to be light and fluffy, and this normally comes from air being beaten into the batter to help encourage a good rise.

There are various different techniques to making cakes, but the two easiest and most popular are the whisking method (Victoria sandwich, pineapple cake and cupcakes) and the all-in-one batter (Earl Grey chocolate fudge cake), so try both and see what's easier for you.

Whether you're a dunker or a cruncher, there should always be a place in your heart for a biscuit. From the archetypal British crispy round biscuit and the American chewy chocolate chip cookie, to crumbly shortbreads, oaty flapjacks and biscuit bars such as brownies, there is a time for all of them – and it's normally around eleven o'clock when your tummy starts growling, or around three o'clock when you need a blood-sugar boost.

If you're not the most confident cook, biscuits are a perfect place to start – you really can't go wrong. There's something deeply satisfying about a batch of hot-out-of-the-oven biscuits, and it is amazing how popular you will become when you start baking!

Cakes & Biscuits Tips & Tricks

CAKES

* Make sure you have preheated your oven to the right temperature before you start, to give your cakes the best possible rise.

* Bake your cake in the middle of the oven. If you make 2 sandwiches, lay them on separate shelves one above the other as centrally as possible.

* Always weigh or measure ingredients properly, as cake-making is a science and will not work unless it's done just so.

* Always use the size of cake tin specified in the recipe, otherwise you may find your cake turns out too flat or too tall.

* When creaming butter and sugar, use electric beaters to make the mixture as pale and creamy as possible. This will add air to the cake mixture.

* Add eggs one by one, beating them in thoroughly before you add the next one.

* If your cake batter splits (curdles), adding flour will usually bring it back together again.

* Fold in the flour gently to avoid knocking out all the air you have just beaten into the mix!

* Don't allow the cake batter to sit for too long before baking, or the raising agent will activate and the mixture will begin to rise.

ESSENTIAL CAKE-MAKING AND BAKING EQUIPMENT

As cake-making is a bit of a science, and some people take to it more than to other types of cooking, it is definitely worth investing in some bits of equipment to make your life easier.

* Large mixing bowls in either plastic, stainless steel or Pyrex

* Wooden spoons for mixing

* Metal spoons for folding

* Spatulas for scraping

* A palette knife

* Measuring jugs

* Sieves

* An electric hand whisk (so much easier than doing it by hand), or, if you're really lucky, a Kitchen Aid table-top mixer

* Scales (electric are most accurate)

* Cake tins in various sizes and styles, but definitely 2 x 20cm sandwich tins and 1 x 22cm springform cake tin, a 22cm square brownie tin and a 24cm loose-bottomed tart case

* A flat baking sheet (or 2)

* A rolling pin

* Biscuit cutters

* A piping bag

* Baking parchment

- ✸ Check to see if the cake is ready by sticking a metal skewer into it. It will come out clean if the cake is done; if there is still uncooked batter on it, the cake is not ready.

- ✸ Do not open the oven door for the first three-quarters of the cooking time, otherwise the cake may sink in the middle.

- ✸ Leave the cake to cool for a good 15 minutes before removing it from its tin.

- ✸ Allow the cake to cool fully before icing it or eating it.

BISCUITS

- ✸ Make sure your oven is well and truly preheated, as biscuits contain a lot of butter, and if the oven is only warm, this will melt before it cooks.

- ✸ Don't handle or re-roll your biscuit dough too much, or your biscuits will become tough and lose any crumbly texture they might have.

- ✸ Use baking sheets with low or no rims to bake your biscuits – trays with edges will trap any steam and give a less crisp result.

- ✸ Arrange the biscuits slightly higgledy-piggledy on the trays so that they have room to spread out, leaving a good 3cm between them.

- ✸ Make sure you chill your biscuits before cooking them, otherwise you may end up with a melted pool of gunge rather than a firm biscuit.

- ✸ Cook your biscuits on baking parchment, as it really helps avoid sticking. Baking paper can sometimes get a bit sticky.

- ✸ Your biscuits will need time to set, so don't be freaked out if they come out of the oven a little soft. As long as they have enough colour and have been cooked for the right time they will set as they cool.

- ✸ Leave the biscuits to set for a couple of minutes on a tray before transferring them to a wire rack.

LINING A CAKE TIN

To start with, get a really good non-stick cake tin. You may not need to line it, but it is always worth doing anyway. First, grease the tin with either butter or oil. Then line the base of the tin with a circle of greaseproof paper, cut to the same circumference as the base. This will work for most cakes, but if making a fruit cake it's worth taking the added precaution of lining the inner circumference of the tin too. So trim a piece of greaseproof to the same depth (and circumference) as the cake and wrap it around the inside of the tin. You can seal this together with a piece of masking tape, but it doesn't really need it.

When making a fruit cake, especially one with a long cooking time, it's a good idea to line the outside of the tin too. This insulates the cake and helps prevent it scorching. I would simply cut a sheet of greaseproof the same depth and circumference as the outside of the tin, tying string round to hold it together or even taping it, again with masking tape.

★ ☆ ICINGS TIPS & TRICKS ☆ ★

Buttercream ICING

To ice a 20cm cake

250g unsalted butter
250g icing sugar
a pinch of salt

Place the butter, icing sugar, flavouring (see below) and salt into a mixing bowl. Using an electric whisk, beat until light and fluffy.

FLAVOURING IDEAS

★ **Vanilla buttercream:** Add the seeds of 1 vanilla pod.

★ **Lemon buttercream:** Add the finely grated zest of 2 unwaxed lemons.

★ **Orange buttercream:** Add the finely grated zest of 2 oranges.

★ **Strawberry buttercream:** Add 2 tablespoons of good sieved strawberry jam and a spot of pink food colouring.

★ **Chocolate buttercream:** Add 250g of melted 70% dark chocolate.

★ **Salted caramel buttercream:** Melt 100g of sugar in a small frying pan until caramelised. Pour in 100ml of double cream and ½ teaspoon of salt and mix until smooth. Leave to cool, then add to the buttercream.

Drizzle ICING

To ice a 20cm cake

250g icing sugar
5 tablespoons water

Place the ingredients in a bowl and whisk until smooth.

★ **For coloured icing:** Add a few drops of your favourite food colour.

★ **For lemon icing:** Swap the water for the same volume of lemon juice and the zest of 1 unwaxed lemon.

★ **For glaze icing:** Omit 1 tablespoon of water.

Chocolate GANACHE ICING

To ice a 20cm cake

250g dark chocolate (70% cocoa solids), broken into pieces
250g double cream

Place the chocolate in a bowl and melt in the microwave for 1 minute. Place the cream in a saucepan and bring up to a bare simmer. Pour the cream over the chocolate and whisk until smooth. Leave to cool, then whisk again before using. Do not cool in the fridge.

WHITE GANACHE ICING
Swap the dark chocolate for the same quantity of good-quality white chocolate.

A good staple MARZIPAN RECIPE

For a 20cm cake

175g golden caster sugar
280g icing sugar, sifted, plus extra for kneading and
   rolling out
450g ground almonds
1 vanilla pod, seeds scraped out
2 free-range eggs, beaten
½ teaspoon orange or lemon juice

Mix the sugars and almonds in a large bowl, and rub in the vanilla seeds. Make a well in the middle and tip in the eggs and citrus juice. Cut the wet ingredients into the dry with a cutlery knife. Dust the surface with icing sugar, then knead the marzipan briefly with your hands to a smooth dough. Don't overdo it, as the paste can get greasy. Add a bit more icing sugar if it seems too wet. Shape into a ball, then wrap and keep in a cool place until ready to cover the cake. Can be made up to 2 days in advance.

MARZIPAN

MARZIPANING & ICING
Christmas or wedding cakes

To ice a 22cm cake

Lift the cake on to a cake board or plate and use a pastry brush to cover evenly with a thin layer of sieved apricot jam. Dust a work surface with more icing sugar and roll the marzipan into a circle about 40cm across, dusting underneath the marzipan with more icing sugar and giving it a quarter turn after every few pushes of the rolling pin to ensure a good circle shape.

Flip the top of the circle back over your rolling pin so you can see the underside of the marzipan, then lift the pin up and lower the marzipan over the cake. Stop once you can see that the edge of the marzipan nearest you is about level with the bottom of the cake. Flop the front of the marzipan down. Smooth the paste over the cake using the palms

of your hands, then trim with a sharp knife. If any cracks appear, simply pinch the paste back together and smooth. Leave to dry for at least 24 hours, or up to 3 days, before covering with icing.

Use a pastry brush to coat the marzipan with another layer of sieved apricot jam.

Dust a work surface with some more icing sugar and roll out 1.25kg of ready-rolled icing. In the same way you placed the marzipan on the cake, use the rolling pin to place the icing. Smooth the icing down and trim the same as the marzipan. Leave to dry for at least a day.

Victoria SPONGE

The simple elegance of a Victoria sandwich makes it a teatime classic and it's no surprise that it's regarded as the queen of cakes! In my opinion, a feather-light sponge like this is the best cake to start practising with. Nail this one and cake-making will become a whole heap easier!

Makes 10 slices
Preparation time 10 minutes
Cooking time 25 minutes

170g softened butter, plus extra for greasing
170g golden caster sugar
3 large free-range eggs
170g self-raising flour
1 teaspoon baking powder
2 tablespoons milk
1 teaspoon vanilla extract
3 tablespoons chunky strawberry jam
150ml double cream, whipped softly
icing sugar, for dusting

Lemon cake: Add the juice and zest of 2 lemons in place of the vanilla extract and 1 tablespoon of milk. Fill the cooked cake with lemon curd instead of jam.

Coffee and walnut cake: Add 1½ tablespoons of espresso powder diluted in 2 tablespoons of boiling water in place of the milk, and stir in 85g of walnut pieces with the flour. Fill and ice with a coffee mascarpone icing, made from 250g of mascarpone mixed with 100ml of double cream and 1 tablespoon of espresso coffee powder diluted in 1 teaspoon of boiling water.

Preheat the oven to 170°C/gas 3. Butter and line two 20cm sandwich cake tins. Place the butter and sugar in a mixing bowl and beat together with an electric whisk for around 5 minutes, or until they become pale and creamy. Whisk in the eggs, one by one, until they are combined (you may find the mixture splits a little when you pop in your last egg).

Sift over the flour and the baking powder and fold them in using a metal spoon. Loosen the mixture with 1 tablespoon of milk and the vanilla extract. You want the batter to fall off the spoon easily, so if you think it's still too thick, stir in the other tablespoon of milk.

Divide the mixture between the sandwich tins and bake for 25 minutes, or until golden and cooked through. You can check this by sliding a skewer into the cake; if it comes out clean it's done.

Leave the cakes to cool in the tins for 15 minutes, then transfer them carefully to a wire rack to cool completely.

If the cakes have rounded tops, carefully cut the rounded part off one of them (this will be the base). Spread this half with the jam, then top with the whipped cream. Sandwich with the other cake, then place a little icing sugar in a small sieve and dust the top. Needless to say, you have to serve this cake with a cup of tea!

Pineapple cake with
LIME-SOURED CREAM FROSTING

I am exposed to all sorts of fantastic foods – I only wish I could describe what it's like walking through Dalston market on a hot day to the smell of overripe pineapples, the inspiration for this cake, which also evokes memories of exotic holidays. I have taken flavours and influences from the Caribbean – fragrant pineapple, sweet cinnamon, tantalising spices and sour limes – and packed them into this cake, which gives flashes of sunshine in every bite.

Makes 10 slices
Preparation time 10 minutes
Cooking time 30 minutes

200g softened butter, plus extra for greasing
200g light muscovado sugar
4 large free-range eggs
200g self-raising flour
1 teaspoon baking powder
1 teaspoon ground cinnamon
1 teaspoon mixed spice
a 225g tin of crushed pineapple or finely
    chopped pineapple chunks, with juice
1 teaspoon vanilla extract
zest and juice of 1 lime

For the lime-soured cream frosting
200ml soured cream
juice and zest of 1 lime, plus extra zest for
    decoration
100g icing sugar
200ml double cream

Preheat the oven to 170°C/gas 3. Grease and line a 20cm springform cake tin. Place the butter and sugar in a mixing bowl and beat together with an electric whisk until pale and fluffy. Add the eggs, one at a time, then sift over the flour, baking powder, cinnamon and mixed spice and stir in. Finally stir in the pineapple, vanilla extract and lime zest and juice.

Pour the cake mixture into the tin, levelling off the top as you go, then pop into the oven and bake for 30 minutes. The cake is ready once you can slide a skewer into it and it comes out clean. Remove the cake from the oven and leave to cool in the tin for 15 minutes, then transfer it carefully to a wire rack to cool completely.

To make the frosting, mix together the soured cream, lime zest and juice and icing sugar. Whip the double cream and gently fold into the soured cream mixture. Ice the top of the cake thickly with the icing, and decorate with lime zest.

Reese's PEANUT BUTTER *cupcakes*

These cupcakes are a twist on the American treats called 'Reese's peanut butter cups' and have turned out to be one of the real gems in this book. An indulgent, peanut-butter-cup-dotted chocolate sponge, piled high with a whipped peanut buttery frosting and sprinkled with more chopped Reese's peanut butter cups – it makes you wonder what they really mean by the American dream! If you cannot find Reese's peanut butter cups, use a Snickers bar chopped up.

Preheat the oven to 170°C/gas 3. Put 18 cupcake cases in the holes of 2 Yorkshire pudding or muffin tins. Place the butter and sugar in a mixing bowl and beat with an electric whisk for around 5 minutes, or until pale and creamy. Whisk in the eggs, one by one, until combined. You may find the mixture curdles a little when you pop in your last egg but it should come together again when you add the flour.

Sift over the flour, cocoa powder and baking powder and stir in. Loosen the mixture with 3 tablespoons of milk and the vanilla extract. You want the batter to fall off the spoon easily; if you think it's too thick, stir in another tablespoon of milk. Stir in the chopped Reese's peanut butter cups.

Divide the mixture between the cupcake cases and bake for 20–25 minutes, or until golden and cooked through. You can check this by sliding a skewer into a cake; if it comes out clean, it's done.

Leave the cakes to cool in the tin for 10 minutes, then transfer them carefully to a wire rack to cool completely.

To make the peanut butter frosting, beat the peanut butter with the icing sugar and cream cheese for a few minutes, or until smooth and creamy. There are no real rules when icing a cupcake except that it has to be thick – really thick – so whether you want to use a knife or piping bag, give them some shape or make them smooth, the choice is yours. Decorate with chopped Reese's peanut butter cups or peanuts.

Makes 18
Preparation time 15 minutes
Cooking time 25 minutes

170g softened butter
170g golden caster sugar
3 large free-range eggs
170g self-raising flour
3 tablespoons cocoa powder
1 teaspoon baking powder
3–4 tablespoons milk
1 teaspoon vanilla extract
6 Reese's peanut butter cups, chopped into small pieces
Reese's peanut butter cups or peanuts, to decorate

For the peanut butter frosting
200g peanut butter
170g icing sugar
150ml full fat cream cheese (Philadelphia is good)

Marbled CHOCOLATE BROWNIES

The ultimate chocolate fix has got to come from a brownie! There are hundreds of brownie recipes out there, but in this one I have used half plain chocolate and half white, swirling them together to make a gooey, extra-chocolatey treat – a chocoholic's dream!

Heat the oven to 180°C/gas 4. Grease and line a 23cm square brownie tin. Break up the chocolate and place in 2 separate Pyrex bowls. Cut the butter in half, then cut each half into cubes. Place half the butter in the bowl with the white chocolate and the other half with the plain. Pop the bowls into the microwave (one at a time) for 1½ minutes, stirring halfway through. White chocolate can be a little tricky to work with, so be patient. It may need another 30 seconds.

Add 150g of the sugar and 2 beaten eggs to each bowl, then sift 70g of the flour into each of the mixes.

Spoon alternate blobs of mixture into the brownie tin to make a patchwork effect. You can be as messy as you like, but try to remember to layer the white chocolate mixture on top of the brown. Once all the mixture is in the tin, use a knife to drag it up and down the length of the tin, then repeat in the other direction. This will make beautiful swirly patterns and give it that lovely marbled finish.

Bake in the oven for 35 minutes. The brownies will be firm on top but you should feel a little bit of give. It needs to be slightly undercooked to get that moist brownie fudginess. Leave to cool completely in the tin, then cut the brownies into 16 squares.

Makes 16 squares
Preparation time 15 minutes
Cooking time 35 minutes

200g white chocolate (use a good-quality one like Green & Black's)
200g plain chocolate (70% cocoa solids)
250g butter
300g golden caster sugar
4 free-range eggs
140g plain flour

Scones

Is it a cake or a biscuit? Who knows, but what is for sure is that no tea party would be complete without scones. They are the highlight of the peculiarly English cream tea, and I can claim to have eaten some of the best in the country, from rustic ones in St Ives to posh ones at the Ritz. As long as they are slathered in clotted cream and strawberry jam (and personally I get as much satisfaction from building them as devouring them) I am one very happy young lady!

Makes 10 scones
Preparation time 10 minutes
Cooking time 12 minutes
Cooling time 15 minutes

55g unsalted butter
225g self-raising flour, plus extra for rolling
1½ tablespoons golden caster sugar
150ml milk
1 free-range egg yolk, whisked, for glazing

Heat the oven to 200°C/gas 6. Place the butter and flour in a food processor and whiz until it begins to look like breadcrumbs. Pour the sugar through the funnel until evenly distributed. Tip the mixture into a mixing bowl, then, using a wooden spoon (or my favourite, your hands), mix in the milk. This will turn it into a soft dough. Knead it enough so it comes together, but do not overwork it or you will get heavy scones.

Flour the work surface and rolling pin. I like big fat scones, so I would roll the dough out about 0.5cm thick. Take a 4 or 5cm pastry cutter and cut out rounds. You should get around 10 scones from each batch. Lay them on a baking sheet and brush the tops with the whisked egg yolk. Bake for 10 minutes, or until risen and golden-brown. Leave to cool for about 15 minutes, and serve them still warm, with clotted cream and jam.

Earl Grey CHOCOLATE FUDGE CAKE

If a Victoria sandwich is the queen of cakes, then chocolate fudge cake has to be the king! Infusing a chocolate cake with a hint of Earl Grey tea adds an aromatic tinge to its fudgy excellence – making it a true object of desire. If you're pushed for time (or inclination), skip the Earl Grey gold dust, but you can see how beautiful it looks and how it turns a simple chocolate cake into a masterpiece.

Makes 10 slices
Preparation time 15 minutes
Cooking time 50 minutes
Cooling time 2 hours
Decorating time 30 minutes

For the cake
6 Earl Grey teabags
150ml boiling water
100g unsalted butter, melted and cooled,
    plus extra butter for greasing
3 large free-range eggs
150g soft dark brown sugar
100g light muscovado sugar
250g self-raising flour
120g plain chocolate (70% cocoa solids),
    melted and cooled
1 teaspoon bicarbonate of soda
1 teaspoon baking powder
3 tablespoons Greek yoghurt

For the Earl Grey cream
4 Earl Grey teabags
100ml boiling water
3 tablespoons light muscovado sugar
250g cream cheese

For the chocolate icing
150g plain chocolate (70% cocoa solids)
100ml double cream
3 tablespoons honey

For the Earl Grey gold dust
2 tablespoons golden caster sugar
1 Earl Grey teabag

Preheat the oven to 180°C/gas 4. To make the cake, place the Earl Grey teabags in a cup and cover with the boiling water. Leave the tea to stew for 5 minutes, then squeeze out the teabags and discard, leaving the really strong tea to cool a little. Grease and line a 20cm springform cake tin with butter and a disc of greaseproof paper. Place all the cake ingredients, including the tea, into a food processor and blend until you have a smooth batter. Pour the batter into the cake tin and level out the surface. Bake in the oven for 50 minutes, or until you can stick a metal skewer into the centre and it comes out clean. Leave to cool in its tin, covered with a clean tea towel, for 2 hours.

To make the Earl Grey cream, place the Earl Grey teabags in a small pan and cover with the boiling water. Leave the tea to stew for 5 minutes, then remove the teabags, squeezing out the liquid as you go. Add the sugar to the tea, bring to the boil and boil for 5 minutes or until syrupy. Leave to cool for 10 minutes then whisk into the cream cheese.

Slice the cooled cake in half horizontally. Cover the bottom half with the Earl Grey cream, then place the top of the cake back on. Melt the chocolate for the icing. Add the double cream and honey, then pour the chocolate icing over the cake. Using a spatula, gently tease the icing around the edges until the whole cake is iced. It looks beautiful if you draw swirls through it.

To make the gold dust, melt the sugar in a small dry frying pan. Once starting to caramelise, empty out the teabag into the caramel and stir the loose tea leaves through. Take off the heat immediately and pour on to a sheet of greaseproof paper. Leave to cool for 10 minutes, then grind up in a pestle and mortar until it becomes golden and dusty. Sprinkle over the top of the cake and serve.

Vanilla BUTTER BISCUITS

On their own these biscuits are divine, but the great thing about them is that the dough is so versatile and makes a great base for all sorts of goodies. Get the basic technique right and you will be able to experiment and create many weird and wonderful concoctions.

Makes 30 biscuits
Preparation time 10 minutes
Chilling time 50 minutes
Cooking time 8 minutes
Cooling time 10 minutes

250g butter, softened
110g golden caster sugar
1 free-range egg yolk
2 teaspoons vanilla extract
300g plain flour

Preheat the oven to 180°C/gas 4. Mix together the butter and sugar in a food processor. Crack in the egg yolk, add the vanilla extract and beat lightly until smooth. Sift in the flour and give it a good whiz. You will find the mixture comes together in a big ball. Pop this into the fridge for 30 minutes.

Shape the mixture into 30 balls and lay on a baking sheet (you may need to bake them in batches). With the palm of your hand, press the balls down one at a time to flatten them. Pop them back into the fridge for another 10 minutes. This dough is very well-behaved and rolls really easily, so if you would like to make shapes with cutters you can have a good play around!

Bake the biscuits in the preheated oven for 8 minutes, or until turning slightly golden. Remove from the oven and leave to cool for 10 minutes, then transfer to a wire rack until completely cold.

Lemony light bites: Add the zest of 2 lemons or swap the vanilla extract for lemon extract. Ice the biscuits, when cold, with lemon drizzle icing made from 110g of icing sugar mixed with the juice and zest of 2 lemons.

Spiced biscuits: Add 1 teaspoon of ground ginger, 1 teaspoon of ground cinnamon and 1 teaspoon of mixed spice to the flour when making the dough.

Almond crumbles: Swap 100g of the flour for chopped almonds and substitute the vanilla extract with almond extract.

Chocolate and hazelnut chip cookies: Add 100g of plain chocolate chips and 50g of chopped hazelnuts to the dough.

Chewy ginger & WHITE CHOCOLATE COOKIES

My big sister Heni is renowned for her cookies, and her recipe is a staple for all the family. I've made my own version by adding ginger and by changing from milk to white chocolate. Cookies (in my opinion) are best served with a glass of milk.

Heat the oven to 180°C/gas 4. Place the butter and sugars into a bowl and whisk until light and fluffy. Add the egg and whisk until combined (sometimes the mixture splits, but don't worry, as the flour will bring it back together).

Add the vanilla extract, ginger, flour and bicarbonate of soda and mix until you have a nice firm dough. With a wooden spoon, fold in the chocolate and ginger pieces. Form into 20 balls and place them on a greased baking sheet. You may need to do this in batches, depending on the size of your baking sheet. Bake for about 10 minutes, or until the cookies have turned golden at the edges. Remove from the oven and leave to cool for 10 minutes, then transfer to a wire rack until completely cold.

Makes about 20 cookies
Preparation time 15 minutes
Cooking time 10 minutes
Cooling time 10 minutes

150g butter, softened
150g light brown sugar
50g dark brown sugar
1 free-range egg
1 teaspoon vanilla extract
1 teaspoon ground ginger
225g plain flour
¾ teaspoon bicarbonate of soda
150g white chocolate, chopped into chunks
1 tablespoon chopped stem ginger

WHY NOT TRY?

Chocolate orange cookies: Leave out the ground ginger and instead add the grated zest of 1 orange. Swap the white chocolate for milk chocolate and add 50g of chopped candied orange peel.

Millionaire's SHORTBREAD
WITH ROSEMARY-INFUSED SALTED *caramel*

The rosemary-salted caramel is revolutionary. You would never think to pair the two ingredients, but rosemary adds a mature depth to this normally too-sweet treat. And the basic shortbread recipe is fantastic on its own too!

Preheat the oven to 170°C/gas 3. Line a 23cm square brownie tin with greaseproof paper. Put the flour and sugar into a bowl and rub in 200g of the butter – the texture will be sandy but malleable enough to form a ball shape when pushed together. Press this sandy shortbread mixture into the tin and smooth it with your knuckles. Prick it with a fork and bake for 5 minutes, then lower the oven temperature to 150°C/gas 2 and cook for a further 30 minutes or until pale golden and no longer doughy. Let it cool in the tin.

Melt the remaining 115g butter in a pan over a low heat for 2–3 minutes, then add the condensed milk, golden syrup and rosemary sprigs. Whisk the mixture well until the butter is thoroughly incorporated. Bring to a slow simmer, then, keeping the temperature even, cook for 10 minutes, stirring continuously, until thickened and light golden brown in colour (this mixture can burn very easily, so never take your eyes off it!). Very carefully remove the rosemary from the pan, then pour the sauce evenly over the cooled shortbread. Sprinkle with the salt and leave it to set.

Break the chocolate into pieces and place in a microwaveable bowl. Microwave for 1 minute, 45 seconds on high, or until fully melted, stirring halfway through. Leave to cool for 5 minutes, then pour and spread the melted chocolate evenly over the toffee mixture and leave to cool in the fridge for 1 hour. Once set, cut the caramel shortbread into 16 squares. The squares can be stored in the fridge, but if you keep them at room temperature for a while the caramel goes lovely and gooey!

Makes 16 squares
Preparation time 15 minutes
Cooking time 35 minutes
Cooling time 1 hour

225g plain flour
85g caster sugar
315g unsalted butter
1 x 397g tin of sweetened condensed milk
4 tablespoons golden syrup
2 sprigs of fresh rosemary
1 teaspoon Maldon sea salt
200g good-quality plain chocolate (at least 70% cocoa solids)

WHY NOT TRY?

Ginger millionaire's shortbread: Add 1 teaspoon of ground ginger to the flour when making the shortbread. Replace the rosemary with 1 tablespoon of chopped stem ginger and 1 tablespoon of the gingery syrup it comes in.

Blond ROCKY ROAD

Traditional rocky road can sometimes be a bit rich, but using white chocolate mixed with coffee gives a milder biscuit that still has an adult edge. These are super for after-dinner coffee biscuits, and fantastic for a mid-morning pick-me-up.

Makes 24 squares
Preparation time 15 minutes
Cooking time 5 minutes
Chilling time 2 hours to overnight

100ml double cream
1 tablespoon instant espresso powder
125g unsalted butter, softened
300g white chocolate, broken into pieces
3 tablespoons honey
200g shortbread
100g mini marshmallows
100g macadamia nuts, toasted
100g fudge, chopped into small cubes

Heat the double cream in a small, heavy-based pan over a low heat. Add the coffee powder and stir until dissolved, then put to one side. In another heavy-based pan, melt together the butter, white chocolate and honey over a gentle heat. Remove from the heat, then transfer one-third of the mixture to another, smaller bowl and set aside to cool. Pour the remainder, along with the coffee cream mixture, into a large mixing bowl.

Place the shortbread in a plastic freezer bag and bash with a rolling pin until you have small pieces. Tip the shortbread pieces, mini marshmallows, macadamia nuts and fudge into the mixing bowl with the other ingredients and mix together well.

Line a 24cm square brownie tin with clingfilm. Pour in the rocky road mixture and level off the surface. Pour on the reserved butter and white chocolate mixture and smooth the surface. Pop it into the fridge and leave to chill for at least 2 hours, or overnight. Lift the clingfilm up to take the biscuits out of the tin, and cut the rocky road into 24 squares to serve. They need to be kept chilled or they can become a bit sticky.

12

BREAD & PASTRY

Many moons ago the main function of pastry was to encase meats and fruits to protect them while cooking, and to make nifty packaging for long journeys or taking to work. The first lunchbox, some might say. Normally the fillings were eaten and the pastry would be thrown away, which seems an awful shame. These days, after refining the pastry-making technique and with a little help from our French neighbours, pastry stands out in its own right and has become one of the core kitchen skills, so much so that there are even chefs dedicated to the art of pastry-making.

The basic make-up of pastry is flour and fat, but there are many different types of pastry. Shortcrust, flaky, puff, filo, choux, suet, hot water crust, almond and sweet French – I have picked the ones that I think will be most useful to learn, and made them a little easier so that they suit the time constraints we all have to deal with these days.

And can you imagine a world without our daily bread? Sadly, bread-making is becoming a skill of the past, which makes no sense to me because I get such satisfaction out of making bread. It makes my mind boggle how the process turns a few humble ingredients into a loaf of bread. And you really can't do better than a homemade loaf, freshly baked. Once you try this yourself, you'll be hooked – I guarantee it.

★ ☆ Bread Tips & Tricks ☆ ★

Bread-making is a lost art and it is actually quite a science too. Grasp a good understanding of it and it'll make a whole heap of sense. Here's the lowdown…

YEAST

For your bread to rise you will need yeast, which, under the right conditions, grows and reproduces to help create a well-risen loaf. But yeast is a sensitive foodstuff: too much of one ingredient can exhaust it, while not enough of something else will deny it the energy it needs to work.

Yeast relies on warmth, moisture and food. Too much heat will kill it – so watch the temperature of the liquid you mix it with: blood temperature is perfect. You also need the right amount of water, or the dough will be heavy and tough and have trouble rising.

Yeast also needs food, and by that I mean sugar and flour proteins, so always add a little sugar (this also enhances the flavour). Some sweet breads call for quite a lot of sugar, which means they can take as long as 5 hours to rise, so don't be freaked out if you don't seem to be getting much movement in your dough. It will go eventually!

There are various types of yeast. Fresh yeast offers the best flavour, but is the hardest to get hold of, although you may find it in bakeries and from the fresh bread counter in supermarkets. Fast-acting dried active yeast is the most common, bought in sachets or tins. Yeast in sachets (usually 7g each) is more powdery and is added straight in with the flour; the more granular yeast from the tin needs to be soaked in water with sugar to be activated. You

will normally need the same amount (about 7g) to raise 500g flour.

I've also included some delicious yeast-free breads: soda bread, cornbread and chapattis, which are all as simple to make as baking a cake.

FLOUR

Strong flour is essential, as it contains more gluten than standard flour – and gluten is the substance that causes bread to become stringy and stretchy, distinguishing the texture of bread from the texture of cake. The flour's gluten is developed when it is mixed with liquid and during kneading.

BREAD

The best bread is made from the best flour, so shop around to find a brand that works for you. One tip is to look for flour from Canada, specifically Manitoba: Canadians tend to produce the best bread flour as a result of their hard winter wheat season, which produces flour with a high level of gluten.

SALT

Unseasoned bread is dreadful, but too much salt will inhibit the bread from rising. One teaspoon of salt per 500g flour tends to work perfectly.

FAT

In order to soften the dough, you need to add a little fat, preferably olive oil or butter. When the yeast has got to work on the gluten-developed dough the fat will stretch the strands of the dough.

THE SIX STAGES OF

Breadmaking

MIXING
The ingredients are combined.

KNEADING
The dough is manipulated to activate the yeast and develop the gluten.

RISING
The dough is left somewhere warm, like an airing cupboard, to rise until it has doubled in size.

KNOCKING BACK AND SHAPING
This is when you push all of the air out of the dough and shape it into a loaf, a pizza or rolls. Great fun!

PROVING
The dough has its second rise.

BAKING
The dough rises to its maximum height during cooking, becomes fluffy and light inside and forms a lovely crust.

★ ☆ PASTRY TIPS & TRICKS ☆ ★

Successful pastry-making needs a cool environment, and this includes kitchen, surfaces, utensils and hands. It is a good idea to put your mixing bowl or food processor bowl and blade in the fridge for an hour before starting.

* Making pastry is an exact science, so make sure you measure everything accurately beforehand.

* As butter is the primary ingredient in most pastry, use the best quality butter you can get your mitts on; this will ensure the best possible taste.

* If holes appear in the pastry when lining a tart dish, just patch them up with any leftover pastry.

* Don't over-mix pastry dough as this will result in tough chewy pastry. You literally need to combine it all together and that's it!

* Let your pastry rest in the fridge for 30 minutes before rolling it out, then let it rest again before baking it. Make sure it's firm before baking, as this will stop the pastry shrinking too much during cooking.

* Always preheat the oven before baking, otherwise the butter will melt before it has cooked and become greasy. This will cause pastry to remain soggy and not seal properly.

LINING A TART CASE

Heat the oven to 180°C/gas 4. Remove the pastry from the fridge and leave to sit for a minute or two. Dust a work surface and the rolling pin with flour and roll out the pastry to the thickness of a 50-pence piece. Keep turning the pastry as you roll it to ensure you get an even circle, as this will make it much easier to line the tart tin.

Fold one end of the pastry over the rolling pin and quickly transfer it to a 22cm loose-based tart tin. It is not necessary to line the base of the tin with greaseproof paper, as there is so much butter in the pastry it is unlikely to stick, but if you're nervous then feel free to do so.

Gently ease the pastry into the corners of the tin and leave any excess pastry overhanging the edge. I prefer to leave the excess pastry folded over the edge of the tart tin and bake it like this, as I find it easier to trim off the edges once the tart has cooked, which gives a neater finish. Leave for 30 minutes; resting helps prevent the pastry from shrinking during baking.

BAKING BLIND

To bake blind, line the raw pastry case with a sheet of greaseproof paper (I find you can get it into the corners much more easily if you crumple the paper first). Fill with either ceramic baking beans (available from cookshops) or dried pulses. Bake in the oven for 25 minutes or until the pastry is cooked through but still has only a little colour, then remove the beans and greaseproof lining and bake for another
5 minutes to guarantee a good snap when the pastry is cut. The edges of the pastry that have been folded over the edge of the tin will turn a bit darker than the rest of the pastry, but they will be trimmed off later, so don't worry.

Keep the pastry case in the tart tin while you leave it to cool for 20 minutes on a wire rack. After this time, use a knife gently to ease the excess pastry away from the edge of the tart tin and neatly level the edges off. The pastry is a bit like Polyfilla at this stage, and more durable than you may think, but you should still be careful while doing this. (If the tart case breaks or splits, try sealing it by painting on some egg wash and popping it back into the oven for a minute or two.) Now you're ready to fill the tart.

Foolproof SHORTCRUST PASTRY

Makes enough to line an 18cm tart tin

Shortcrust pastry used to be my biggest food nemesis, as it was always either too short and crumbly, falling apart when I tried to line a tart tin, or too tough and chewy. Finding the right shortness and creating pastry with a crisp buttery texture can give even the most confident cook the heebie-jeebies. But I've discovered the secret: by adding an egg to your pastry instead of water you will guarantee crispness every time and find it much easier to roll – I've not had a pastry nightmare since.

Preparation time 10 minutes
Resting time 30 minutes

225g plain flour
a pinch of salt
120g ice-cold butter, cubed
1 free-range egg, whisked

Place the flour in a food processor with the salt and whiz for a few seconds (this is a great way of ditching the arduous process of sifting flour). Add the butter and whiz again for about 20 seconds, or until the mixture resembles breadcrumbs.

Turn out into a fridge-cold mixing bowl (it helps prevent the butter melting) and, with a cold knife, mix in the whisked egg: this will bind the mixture together.

Bind the pastry into a ball. Kneading will make it tough, so try to handle the pastry as little as possible. Lay the pastry on a baking sheet and roll out to flatten a little (this makes it easier to roll later on). Cover with clingfilm and leave in the fridge to rest for at least 30 minutes or until needed.

SEX IT UP

To make sweet shortcrust: Add 1 tablespoon icing sugar in with the flour.

To make herb pastry: Add 1 tablespoon of chopped fresh herbs with the flour and butter at the breadcrumb stage.

To make cheese pastry: Add 1 tablespoon of grated Parmesan cheese and a pinch of cayenne pepper with the flour.

Almond PASTRY

Makes enough to line an 18cm tart tin

The richest of pastries, but also the naughtiest! Yet this is the easiest pastry to make and work with, as it is so flexible. It makes delicious biscuits too.

Preparation time 10 minutes
Resting time 30 minutes

225g plain flour
a pinch of salt
85g ground almonds
170g unsalted butter
85g icing sugar
1 free-range egg
2–3 drops of vanilla extract

Place all the ingredients in a food processor and blitz until the dough just comes together (if you mix it too much it will become tough).

Bind the pastry into a ball. Kneading will make it tough, so try to handle the pastry as little as possible. Lay the pastry on a baking sheet and roll out to flatten a little (this makes it easier to roll later on). Cover with clingfilm and leave in the fridge to rest for 30 minutes or until needed.

Cheat's FLAKY PASTRY

Makes 450g pastry

Puff pastry is such a bore to make that I chose not to include it in this book – in any case, you can buy great-quality, ready-made, all-butter puff pastries, so why bother? But there is something about making a pastry that rises that is good for the soul, and flaky pastry does just that, in pretty much the same time as it takes to make a simple shortcrust. Make sure you keep everything as cold as possible so that the butter stays firm and doesn't melt!

Preparation time 10 minutes
Resting time 30 minutes

225g plain flour
½ teaspoon salt
170g unsalted butter, kept in the freezer for 1 hour
120ml ice-cold water

Sift the flour into a bowl with the salt. Using a large-holed cheese grater, grate in the butter as fast as you can so that it doesn't melt. Take a metal knife and delicately coat the butter strands in flour until all the strands are coated and the butter is spread evenly throughout the flour. Add the ice-cold water and bind together with the knife.

On a floured surface, bring the pastry together into a ball. Try not to handle it too much, as you want to keep the butter strands from melting and handling pastry too much makes it tough.

Roll the pastry into a long oblong, then fold one third over into the centre of the pastry and the other third over the top of that. Cover in clingfilm and leave to rest in the fridge for 30 minutes or until needed.

SEX IT UP

Cheese flaky pastry: Add 55g of grated Parmesan cheese and a pinch of cayenne pepper with the flour at the beginning.

Sweet flaky pastry: Add 2 tablespoons of icing sugar with the flour at the beginning.

CHOUX PASTRY TIPS & TRICKS

✳ Make sure the dough is cool enough to touch before you put the eggs in, otherwise the eggs will cook and your choux pastry won't rise very well.

✳ Don't beat the flour, butter and water together too much, otherwise you will get lots of little cracks all over the surface of the pastry and the buns will be a bit tough.

✳ Make sure the oven is really hot before baking choux pastry so that you get the best possible chance of a good rise.

✳ Don't open the door of the oven while the pastry is cooking, as this will inhibit its ability to rise.

Choux PASTRY
Makes 300g

Choux pastry is that light puffy pastry traditionally used for choux buns, éclairs and profiteroles. It had a reputation for being hard work, as you need to use serious elbow grease when making it by hand, but if you have electric beaters you can throw it together in minutes without breaking a sweat. The result is little pillowy buns that are crisp on the outside but so light in the middle.

Preparation time 15 minutes
Cooling time 10 minutes
Cooking time 30 minutes

90g butter
110g plain flour
pinch of salt
3 large free-range eggs

Melt the butter and 220ml water together in a pan, then turn the heat up and bring to the boil. When the water is starting to creep up the sides of the pan and just starting to roll over, pour in the flour and salt as quickly as possible, then whisk with a balloon whisk: the mixture will gradually start to come away from the edges of the pan and form a doughy ball.

SEX IT UP

Cheese choux buns: Add 55g of chopped Parmesan cheese and a pinch of cayenne pepper with the flour and shape into small golf balls.

Profiteroles: Shape a batch of choux pastry into small rounds, about the size of golf balls, then fill with 290ml of whipped sweetened cream or crème patissière. Divide between plates and cover with chocolate sauce (page 248) to serve.

Tip the ball of pastry into a mixing bowl and leave to cool for 10 minutes. Break one egg into the bowl and, using an electric whisk, beat together the egg and the paste until combined. Repeat with the remaining 2 eggs. You should be left with a smooth paste that drops from a spoon reluctantly and without splatting as it hits the surface.

Line a baking sheet with baking parchment. Pour the paste into a piping bag (or use a spoon for profiteroles or choux buns if you like). Pipe shapes on to the parchment, leaving enough room around each bun for it to rise (they will double in size). Aim for chipolata shapes for éclairs, small golf balls for profiteroles and plum-sized blobs for choux buns.

Preheat the oven to 200°C/gas 6. Pop the baking sheet into the oven and bake the choux pastry for 20–25 minutes, or until the buns are risen and golden and hollow if you tap them. Remove them from the oven and, using a metal skewer, pierce the bottom of each bun, then turn them upside down and return them to the oven for 5 minutes. This will dry the middles out, making them perfect for filling. Remove from the oven and leave to cool.

FILLING A CHOUX BUN
Fit the thinnest nozzle on a piping bag, then fill the piping bag with your chosen choux bun filling. The holes that you made in the bottom of your buns in order for the middles to dry out during the cooling process are perfect as entry holes when filling. Stick the nozzle into the hole. Don't worry if the end of the nozzle is not big enough, just wiggle it around a bit until it fits, then squeeze the filling out into the bun. You know the buns are full when the filling starts to push its way back out of the opening. Wipe any excess from the buns then place them, filling side down, on to a tray ready to ice.

Basic white LOAF *plus* 2 VARIATIONS

A basic bread recipe is a saviour in so many ways. Once you have it in your cookery repertoire you will be able to turn your hand to making pizzas, rolls, croissants and brioche, amongst other things. It bothers me that so few of us have ever made our own bread – it's such common food and the stuff we buy off the shelves now is barely representative of the real thing as it's packed full of all sorts of preservatives and nasties.

Put the yeast and sugar into a bowl, cover with the tepid water and leave to one side for 5 minutes. In a bowl (or even better, a mixer or breadmaker), add the flour, the yeast and sugar solution, salt and olive oil.

Mix together to form a soft dough. If making the bread by hand, turn the dough out on to a floured surface, then with a firm fist (dusted with flour to prevent sticking), knead the dough for 10 minutes, pushing and folding the dough over and over again until it springs back when you prod it. This can be quite knackering, but do keep it up as it's the kneading that changes the texture from cake-like to bread-like. (If you're doing this in a mixer, simply switch it on for 10 minutes; if using a breadmaker, just switch it on to the dough setting, where it will both knead the dough and give it its first rise!)

Place the dough in a large, clean mixing bowl which has had a dribble of oil wiped over it. Cover with oiled clingfilm and leave in a warm place, such as an airing cupboard or near a warm cooker, for 1 hour, until doubled in size.

Remove the clingfilm and stick your fist into the dough to knock all the air out of it – a really satisfying feeling! Knock the dough around for a minute, or until it has deflated, then shape it into an oval and pop it into an oiled loaf tin; alternatively, make a large round farmhouse loaf or shape the dough into rolls.

Leave the bread to double again in size, which will take 30–45 minutes. Meanwhile, preheat the oven to 200ºC/gas 6. Place the loaf in the oven and bake for 30–40 minutes until it has risen, become golden and sounds hollow when you tap the base. Leave to cool completely on a wire rack before serving.

Makes 1 good-sized loaf

Preparation time 20 minutes
Rising time 1 hour
Proving time 30–40 minutes
Baking time 30–40 minutes

1 x 7g sachet of fast-acting yeast or
   2 teaspoons dried active yeast
1 teaspoon golden caster sugar
285ml tepid water
500g strong white bread flour, plus extra for
   dusting and rolling
1 teaspoon sea salt
2 tablespoons olive oil, plus extra for oiling

WHY NOT TRY?

Wholemeal bread: To make wholemeal bread replace half the flour (250g) with strong wholemeal bread flour. A loaf made only with wholemeal flour tends to be quite heavy, but by all means give it a go and see if you like it.

Fruit bread: Swap the olive oil for the same quantity of melted butter and add 1 tablespoon of mixed spice with the flour. Once the dough has risen for the first time, knead in 200g of mixed dried fruit before shaping the bread. You may find that it takes a little bit longer to prove, due to the added fruit.

Soda BREAD

If you really don't have the time or the inclination to be dealing with yeast, there are some fantastic yeast-free breads that give the same satisfaction as the yeasty version. The cross on the top of a loaf of soda bread is wonderful, as it is said to let the fairies out. Soda bread is best eaten on the day you make it.

Makes 1 loaf
Preparation time 10 minutes
Cook time 35 minutes

250g plain white flour, plus extra for dusting
250g plain wholemeal flour
100g porridge oats
1 teaspoon bicarbonate of soda
1 teaspoon salt
25g butter, cut into pieces
500ml buttermilk

Preheat the oven to 200ºC/gas 6 and dust a baking sheet with flour. Place the flours, porridge oats, bicarbonate of soda and salt in a food processor. Add the butter and mix until 'rubbed in'. Add the buttermilk through the funnel while the machine is running, then turn off straight away (it is really important you do not over-mix the dough). Bring the dough together very lightly with your fingertips (handle it very, very gently). Now shape it into a flat, round loaf measuring 20cm in diameter.

Place the loaf on the baking sheet and score a deep cross in the top. Bake for 30–35 minutes, until the bottom of the loaf sounds hollow when tapped. If it isn't ready after this time, turn it upside down on the baking sheet and bake for a few minutes more.

Transfer it to a wire rack, cover with a clean tea towel (this keeps the crust nice and soft) and leave to cool. Serve sliced, with unsalted butter.

WHY NOT TRY?

Seeded soda bread: Add 2 tablespoons of mixed seeds to the mixture. I love poppy seeds, sesame seeds and pumpkin seeds.

Chilli & ROSEMARY CORNBREAD

I had to give up wheat temporarily a while back and it was hell. I am a big carbs person and really love bread. Cornbread was my saviour. Not only does it genuinely feel bready, it's got an amazing texture that is superb for scooping up sauces and is a winner with chilli con carne or toasted with melted cheese. It's as easy to bake as a cake, but it's savoury, so feels nothing like one. I have studded it with chilli and rosemary, which infuse into the bread, but have a play around with flavours and see what concoctions you can come up with…

Makes 1 cornbread
Preparation time 15 minutes
Cooking time 25 minutes
Cooling time 10 minutes

50g butter, plus extra for greasing
1 small onion, peeled and finely chopped
570ml low-fat bio yoghurt
2 free-range eggs, whisked
225g fine cornmeal or polenta
140g plain flour
2 teaspoons baking powder
1 teaspoon sea salt
1 teaspoon sugar
2 sprigs of fresh rosemary, each cut into 4
1 red chilli, cut into 8

Preheat the oven to 230ºC/gas 8. Grease a 30cm cake tin or ovenproof frying pan. Melt the 50g of butter in a pan. Tip in the onion and cook over a gentle heat for 5 minutes, until softened and beginning to turn golden.

Beat together the yoghurt and eggs in a separate bowl, then stir in the buttery onions. Mix the cornmeal, flour, baking powder, salt and sugar together in a bowl, then pour over the yoghurt and egg mixture. Stir together until just combined and you have a batter.

Pour the batter into the cake tin or frying pan and smooth the top with a knife. Spear each piece of chilli through the soft centre with a piece of rosemary and place them in the batter, leaving a few centimetres between them. Bake for 25 minutes, until the top is golden and a skewer inserted in the centre comes out clean. Cool in the pan for 10 minutes, then turn out, cut into wedges and serve.

WHY NOT TRY?

Plain cornbread: You don't need to add anything to the basic cornbread recipe – even without the chilli and rosemary, it will still be delicious.

Roasted garlic and rosemary cornbread: Replace each slice of chilli with a roasted garlic clove for a highly aromatic cornbread.

Chapattis

A chapatti is such a classic bread but it often gets overlooked in recipe books. The great thing about it is that it is yeast-free, which means it can be made to order in minutes. Although a conventional Indian bread, a chapatti works wonderfully with a number of cuisines. Try it in place of pitta or a wrap, or serve chapattis the classic way with your favourite curries.

Makes 4
Preparation time 5 minutes
Resting time 5 minutes
Cooking time 10 minutes

100g wholemeal flour, plus extra for rolling
pinch of salt
70ml lukewarm water
2 teaspoons vegetable oil
1 tablespoon melted butter or ghee

Put the flour and salt into a mixing bowl. Pour over the water and bring together with your fingers to form a dough. Knead in the bowl for a few minutes, until the dough feels smooth, soft and flexible, then cover with clingfilm and leave to rest for 5 minutes.

Cut the dough into 4 even-sized pieces and roll each piece into a ball. Flour a work surface and, using a rolling pin, roll each ball into a flat disc, around 20cm in diameter. Make sure you cover them with a clean tea towel so that they do not dry out.

Heat a large frying pan to a medium heat, then wipe half a teaspoon of vegetable oil around the pan with a piece of kitchen paper. Lay a chapatti on the pan and wait for 30 seconds, or until it starts to show little brown spots, then flip it over. Do the same on the other side then flip over again. This time if you press the chapatti gently you will see that it starts to puff up. Flip it over again and let it puff up as much as it can before laying it on a plate and brushing it with some butter or ghee. Repeat with the next 3 chapattis and serve warm.

Horlicks MALT LOAF

Malt loaf is a small, dark fruity loaf so soft that you have to be careful when you cut it, otherwise you will squash it. Crammed full of sultanas and with a syrupy Guinness-like tang, it is sticky and caramelly and clings to your teeth in the same way toffee does. I have quite cleverly (if I do say so myself) added everyone's favourite malt drink to make it extra malty and, in turn, extra moreish. The addition of Horlicks produces a paler loaf, but it is a classic malt loaf in every other way. Sink your teeth into a slice that has been slathered in unsalted butter.

Place the flour, salt, yeast and sultanas in a mixing bowl.

Place the sugar in a jug and top up with warm water to the 225ml mark. Stir the sugar and water together and pour into a small pan, along with the Horlicks, treacle and butter. Melt it all together over a low heat or until it shows its first bubble. Leave on one side until cool enough to touch.

Add the syrup to the flour in the mixing bowl and mix to a soft, sticky dough (it will be much looser than conventional bread dough). Spoon the dough into 2 small oiled loaf tins, cover with a piece of oiled clingfilm and leave in a warm place to rise. As there is so much sugar in the recipe you will find that it's quite a slow rise; it should take around 2 hours, but on a cold day I've known it to take about 5 hours.

Preheat the oven to 190ºC/gas 5. Bake the malt loaf in the oven for 40 minutes, until it sounds hollow when tapped on the base. Leave to cool in the tin for 10 minutes, then transfer to a wire rack to cool completely. Brush the loaf with malt syrup or honey while it is cooling to give you that really gooey coating.

Makes 2 small loaves
Preparation time 5 minutes
Rising time 2 hours
Cooking time 40 minutes

400g plain flour
1 teaspoon salt
1 x 7g sachet fast-acting yeast, or 2 teaspoons dried active yeast
225g sultanas
1 tablespoon brown sugar
4 tablespoons Horlicks
1 tablespoon black treacle
30g unsalted butter
1 tablespoon malt syrup or honey
malt syrup or honey, to glaze

Chocolate, ALMOND & PEAR TART

Almonds, chocolate and pears marry beautifully, and you have a great short-cut here in the form of tinned pears. By simply adding 1 tablespoon of cocoa powder to the pastry mixture, you get a deep chocolatey flavour and colour.

Makes 10 slices
Preparation time 20 minutes
Cooking time 40 minutes

55g plain flour
85g ground almonds
115g golden caster sugar
115g butter, softened
4 large free-range eggs
250g plain chocolate, melted and cooled for
    10 minutes
2 tablespoons Amaretto liqueur (optional)
½ teaspoon vanilla extract
1 quantity almond pastry (see page 211), made
    with 1 tablespoon cocoa powder, baked blind
    in a 22cm tart case (see page 210)
1 x 400g tin of pears, drained (around 6 pear
    halves)
crème fraîche, to serve (optional)

Preheat the oven to 200°C/gas 6. Place the flour, ground almonds, sugar, butter, eggs, melted chocolate, Amaretto (if using) and vanilla extract in a food processor and blend until it has all combined to form a batter. Pour the batter into the tart case and lay the pears neatly on top, pushing them down firmly as you go.

Pop the tart into the oven and bake for 30 minutes, or until the tart looks firm on top and the pears are surrounded by gooey chocolate. You really want to undercook it a little, as it will set more while cooling and it is delicious if it's a bit gooey at the bottom. Remove from the oven and leave to cool. Serve warm or cold, on its own or with crème fraîche.

CHEAT

If you don't have time to make the pastry, buy a good-quality all-butter (preferably organic) pastry case.

Churros with CHOCOLATE SAUCE

On holidays in Spain we always had churros for breakfast. These fluffy morsels are often compared to doughnuts, but they are, in fact, from the choux pastry family. You must eat them piping hot – so your fingers burn when trying to douse them with cinnamon sugar before plunging them into warm chocolate sauce. Kids love them, but I think they make the most fantastic accompaniment to a good cup of coffee.

Pour enough oil into a deep pan to come one-third of the way up the sides (any higher and it could overflow if too hot, which would be very dangerous). Heat it to 180°C (if you don't have a thermometer, a croûton-sized piece of bread needs to turn golden in exactly 20 seconds).

Put the uncooked choux pastry into a piping bag and squeeze directly into the oil in 6cm strips (they look really pretty if you use the star-shaped nozzle!). Do 6 strips at a time. Cook them for 2 minutes, turning occasionally, then remove with a slotted spoon and drain on kitchen paper. Repeat with the rest of the mixture, keeping the cooked ones warm and crisp by placing them in an oven preheated to 180°C/gas 4, with the door slightly open.

Mix together the sugar and cinnamon and toss the churros in it, making sure they get completely covered.

To make the sauce, melt together the chocolate, cream and honey in the microwave for 2 minutes, stirring every so often.

Pour the chocolate sauce into a dipping bowl and serve the churros alongside.

Serves 4
Preparation time 5 minutes
Cooking time 10 minutes

500ml vegetable oil
1 quantity uncooked choux pastry
  (see page 213)
2 tablespoons golden caster sugar
2 teaspoons ground cinnamon

For the sauce
50g dark chocolate (70% cocoa solids)
200ml double cream
2 tablespoons runny honey

Apple & ELDERFLOWER TART

Is it possible to improve on a classic apple tart? Well, I put it to the test and I think I've managed it. The sticky sweetness of elderflower cordial adds a fragrance that is spot on with the tartness of an apple.

Preheat the oven to 180°C/gas 4. Line a 22cm tart tin with pastry and place in the fridge to chill for 10 minutes.

Take 3 of the apples and chop them into small chunks. Pop them into a small pan with 3 tablespoons of the elderflower cordial and cook over a low heat for 10 minutes, or until the apples have softened and begun to break up. You can now either purée the apples in a food processor or, my preference, mash them with a potato masher to get more texture. Leave to cool for 30 minutes.

Cut the remaining apples into thin slivers and mix them with the rest of the cordial. Tip the cooled, stewed apples into the pastry case and carefully arrange the apple slivers on top – you can get creative here with some beautiful patterns! Sprinkle with the sugar, then drizzle with the melted butter and bake in the oven for 45 minutes.

Leave the tart to cool for 20 minutes, then glaze it with the apricot and elderflower mixture. Eat immediately, with ice cream or clotted cream – yum!

Makes 10 slices
Preparation time 20 minutes
Cooking time 1 hour
Cooling time 50 minutes

1 quantity foolproof shortcrust pastry (see page 211)
6 Golden Delicious apples, peeled and cored
4 tablespoons elderflower cordial
1 tablespoon golden caster sugar
3 tablespoons unsalted butter, melted
100g apricot jam, mixed with 1 tablespoon elderflower cordial
ice cream or clotted cream, to serve

Chicken, LEEK & HAM *pies*

My younger sister, Cora, is a chicken pie connoisseur. I am not sure if it is possible for her to turn down a chicken pie if it is on the menu, and it was the first recipe she asked my advice on. This recipe is special to me, as it is something we have honed together – a real Erskine special – and I hope you get as much pleasure out of it as we have.

Serves 4
Preparation time 15 minutes
Cooking time 45 minutes

2 tablespoons butter
3 leeks, finely sliced
3 garlic cloves, peeled and finely chopped
2 tablespoons flour
100ml white wine
400ml chicken stock
50ml double cream
2 chicken breasts, chopped into bitesize pieces
200g cooked ham ends (from the deli counter)
a few sprigs of fresh thyme, leaves picked
1 tablespoon chopped fresh parsley
flour, for dusting
1 quantity cheat's flaky pastry (see page 212)
1 large free-range egg yolk
sea salt and freshly ground black pepper

Fisherman's pies: Swap the chicken and ham for the same quantity of raw mixed fish and seafood. I would go for coley or pollock, salmon, smoked haddock and prawns. Swap the chicken stock for fish stock.

Melt the butter in a medium pan. Add the leeks and cook over a low heat for 10 minutes, or until softened. For the last minute of cooking time, add the garlic. Tip in the flour and cook for a minute, then add the white wine, chicken stock and cream and simmer for 1 minute before adding the chicken and ham. Simmer for 5 minutes, until the chicken is just cooked through, but not over-cooked, and the sauce has thickened. Stir in the thyme and parsley and season to taste.

Divide the chicken mixture between 4 individual pie dishes and leave to cool for 10 minutes. Meanwhile, flour a work surface and roll out the pastry. Using your pie dishes as templates, cut out 4 lids big enough to cover each one. You really don't need to be a neat freak when making your lid – I actually think the more wonky the lid, the better.

Preheat the oven to 200°C/gas 6. Using a pastry brush, paint egg yolk round the edge of each pie dish and top with a pastry lid. Pierce each lid with a skewer and paint more egg yolk all over the lids. Pop them into the fridge for 10 minutes (or all day if you like), then bake them in the oven for 20 minutes, or until the pastry is cooked through and lovely and crisp and the chicken is bubbling away inside.

Super-duper SAUSAGE *rolls*

We all love a good sausage roll, but making them from scratch makes an unbeatable difference to the whole eating experience. They are truly spectacular. And what's really nice with these ones is that you can fill each roll with your favourite chutney or even ketchup for the kids before baking. So you get a lovely oozy sauce with each bite.

Place the sausagemeat into a mixing bowl and add the grated onion, sage, Parmesan (if using), salt, pepper and a light grating of nutmeg.

Dust a work surface with flour and roll out the pastry into an oblong shape with the thickness of a 50-pence piece. Cut the pastry into 3 wide strips and spread 1 tablespoon of your chosen chutney or sauce along each strip.

Divide the sausagemeat mixture into 3 and form into 3 long sausages the same length as the pastry strips. Lay them on the pastry and seal whatever pastry edges are still visible with the beaten egg. Now fold the sausages up in the pastry. Turn them over on to the folded side and carry on glazing the rolls with the egg. Make lots of little slashes on the surface of the rolls with a small knife, then pop them into the fridge for 30 minutes.

Heat the oven to 200°C/gas 6. Place the sausage rolls on a board and cut them into individual rolls, cutting each long roll either into 3 or into lots of small, bite sized rolls. Pop them on to a baking sheet and bake in the oven for 20 minutes for the small ones, 30 minutes for the larger ones.

Remove from the oven and leave to cool for 10 minutes. I think they are just wonderful eaten hot, but they're equally delicious eaten cold the next day.

Makes 9 sausage rolls or lots of smaller ones
Preparation time 30 minutes
Chilling time 30 minutes
Cooking time 20–30 minutes

450g good-quality pork sausagemeat or
   1 x 450g pack of 8 sausages, the meat
   squeezed out from the casings
1 medium onion, peeled and grated
2 sprigs of fresh sage, leaves chopped
1 tablespoon grated Parmesan cheese
   (optional)
sea salt and freshly ground black pepper
fresh nutmeg
flour, for dusting
1 quantity flaky pastry (see page 212)
4 tablespoons of your favourite chutney
   or sauce (I love my Christmas Chutney,
   page 256)
1 large free-range egg, lightly beaten

WHY NOT TRY?

Serving them hot as a main course with mashed potato and onion gravy (see pages 74 and 236).

Beef WELLINGTON

In our house, beef Wellington is the number-one requested dish. People think it's hard to pull off, but in actual fact, other than it being a bit fiddly to roll the pastry out, it is really easy to make. I've given it a glamorous twist with a lug of truffle oil and a wrapping of Parma ham. Try it – you will be so proud of yourself!

Serves 8
Preparation time 40 minutes
Chilling time 1 hour
Cooking time 1 hour

1kg (or a 25cm long piece) beef fillet, taken
    from the middle to thick end
sea salt and freshly ground black pepper
2 tablespoons olive oil
2 banana shallots, peeled and finely chopped
5 field or Portobello mushrooms, finely
    chopped
3 garlic cloves, peeled and finely chopped
a few sprigs of fresh thyme, leaves picked
1 teaspoon truffle oil (optional)
½ small bunch of flat-leaf parsley, chopped
12 slices of Parma ham
flour, for dusting
1 quantity cheat's flaky pastry (see page 212)
2 large free-range egg yolks, beaten

Venison en croûte: Swap the beef for venison fillet. As venison tends to be a bit thinner, I would reduce the cooking time by 5 minutes.

Lay the beef fillet on a board and season heavily with salt and lots of black pepper. Heat 1 tablespoon oil in a frying pan and brown the meat all over for about 8 minutes. Set aside to cool. Heat the other tablespoon of oil and add the shallots to the same pan and sauté for 2 minutes. Add the mushrooms and fry for 10 minutes, or until they have softened and gone brown. For the last minute of cooking, add the garlic, thyme, truffle oil (if using) and parsley. Remove from the heat and leave to cool for 10 minutes.

Lay out a double layer of clingfilm about 40cm long. Then lay another double layer of clingfilm above it, overlapping the first by about 10cm so you have a large rectangular grid of film. Starting at the bottom lay 6 slices of Parma ham centrally, overlapping each slice with the next. Lay the next 6 slices in the same way above this layer to double the width. Spread the mushrooms over the ham. Place the beef at one end of the ham and mushrooms then, with the help of the clingfilm, roll the beef in the ham. Wrap the clingfilm round the beef and roll it tight, tying the ends like a cracker. Pop into the fridge for 30 minutes.

Dust a work surface with flour. Remove the pastry from the fridge, lay it on the floured surface, then roll out into a rectangle measuring 40 x 30cm. Unravel the ham-wrapped beef carefully from its clingfilm. With the widest side of the pastry towards you, lay the beef at the bottom edge of the pastry. Roll the beef in the pastry. Trim off any excess from the sides and tuck the pastry under the beef.

Cut excess pastry into patterns such as leaves or stars. Using a pastry brush, brush the beaten egg yolk over the pastry. Place the pastry shapes on top of the pastry and brush with more egg. Pop the beef Wellington into the fridge for 30 minutes and then preheat the oven to 200°C/gas 6.

Remove from the fridge and bake in the oven for 35 minutes, or until the pastry is golden and crisp, which indicates that the beef is cooked through and will be medium rare. Leave to rest for 15 minutes before serving.

The foundation of cooking, as far as I'm concerned, lies in knowing how to nail a bloody good sauce. That sauce can be a simple tomato sauce or gravy, maybe a jolly good chutney to serve with a pork pie, or you can raise your game and hit your pals with a restaurant-quality jus.

A good sauce can change a simple meal into something special. Take a grilled salmon steak. Delicious on its own, sure, but pair it with a creamy citrus hollandaise and we're talking gourmet. And can you imagine how dull sausages and mash would be without lashings of onion gravy?

The problem is that there are so many things we don't cook ourselves today, and sauces, jams and preserves are what we tend most to cheat on. Even the best chefs will have a jar of Hellmann's at the back of the fridge, and does anyone under 60 make jam?

Well, I do, so let me tell you – it tastes a whole heap better. And spending the afternoon making a chutney or jam is not only therapeutic but a marvellous way to use up fruit or veg that might be on its way out.

Going back to the ready-made sauces, I am ready to protest against Bisto. I'm sorry, those of you who were brought up on the stuff, but it's gross. And you can make proper gravy just as easily, with just the juices left in a roasting tray and some stock.

So whether it be learning to make a good gravy or a beurre blanc, it's all here. I hope I haven't missed out any of your favourites, and I also hope I have convinced you that the real deal is where it's at!

★ ☆ TIPS & TRICKS ☆ ★

SAUCES

* Use a non-stick, heavy-based saucepan, especially when making a milk-based sauce, to prevent burning or curdling.

* Use the best ingredients you can get hold of – a good-quality wine makes a great sauce.

* Although some shop-bought stocks are good, nothing beats a homemade stock for a rich, sticky sauce.

* For a really glossy sauce, whisk through a little butter minutes before serving.

* Make sure your sauce has been properly strained to remove any cooking residue such as bones, whole spices, or vegetables.

* Use only double or whipping cream at high temperatures, because single cream will split.

* Always make sure your sauce is well seasoned, as it can be an integral part of a dish.

* Take advantage of 'cheffy' short cuts by discovering ready-made demi-glaces in top delis or on the internet.

BUTTER SAUCES

* Always use super-fresh eggs at room temperature.

* Unsalted butter is best.

* Use a ceramic, glass or stainless steel bowl to mix the sauce, as copper and aluminium can oxidise with eggs and vinegar.

* Have cold water and a cold bowl to hand in case the sauce splits and you need to rescue it.

* Butter sauces don't keep very well, so make your sauce just before serving, if possible. If your sauce overheats it may curdle: if so, just beat in a splash of cold water and pour the sauce into a cold bowl.

THICKENING SAUCES

★ **Roux:** By starting your sauce with a roux, you will be able to regulate the thickness from the start. A roux is equal quantities of butter and flour melted together and cooked for a minute so that the flour doesn't taste raw, before adding the liquid. This is usually done with gravies or white sauces.

★ **Reducing:** The best way to thicken a liquid is to boil it over a high heat until it has reduced. This also intensifies the flavour.

★ **Beurre manié (moulded butter):** A mixture of equal quantities of butter and plain flour that has been whizzed in a food processor to form a thick paste. This is whisked in to thicken sauces at the end of their cooking time. It's a good method to use if reducing the sauce would make it too strong.

★ **Slaking with cornflour:** Mixing cornflour with a little of the sauce, then stirring it back into the sauce, is an excellent way of thickening a sauce and great for Chinese cooking.

★ **Arrowroot:** Same as cornflour, but used in Western cooking to thicken.

★ **Egg yolks:** These can be used to thicken your sauce, but they must be whisked in very quickly and not overcooked, otherwise they will scramble. Typically used in carbonara sauces or custard.

★ **Monter au beurre:** Whisking in butter at the last minute will thicken a sauce slightly once it's fully emulsified. It also gives the sauce a lovely sheen.

* If it only splits slightly, start again by slowly adding the split sauce to a new egg yolk.

* If your sauce is not thick enough, either you did not beat it vigorously enough, the mixture was not hot enough or you added too much liquid.

* If your sauce looks too oily, simply add a little water or more of the reduction.

MAYONNAISE

* Make sure you use the best ingredients you can get your hands on. Mayonnaise is quite pure, and you will be able to tell if you have not used the best-quality ingredients such as the freshest free-range eggs.

* All the ingredients should be at room temperature.

* If your mayonnaise is too thick and oily, add 1 teaspoon vinegar or water to cut through it and thin it out.

* If your mayonnaise splits or curdles, you have added the oil too quickly, the mayonnaise wasn't beaten fast enough or the ingredients were too cold.

* To rescue curdled mayonnaise, start again by whisking the curdled mixture very slowly into a new egg yolk. Adjust all the seasonings accordingly.

* You can store your mayonnaise, sealed, in the fridge for a week.

WHAT I CAN DO IF MY SAUCE ISN'T RIGHT?

* **Bland:** If your sauce is bland, try increasing the salt quantity and adding some finely ground black pepper or something acidic like lemon juice.

* **Too sweet:** If your sauce is too sweet, add a pinch of salt and regulate it with some vinegar.

* **Too creamy:** If your sauce is too creamy, try thinning it with either water or white wine vinegar.

* **Too acidic:** If it's too acidic, add some cream.

* **Not sure:** If it just isn't rounded off at the edges and you can't put your finger on what's wrong, add ½ teaspoon of sugar or a little redcurrant jelly to bring more depth.

* **Too strong:** If your sauce is too strong, try diluting it with some water. If it becomes too thin you could always 'monter au beurre' (see opposite).

* **Not enough:** If you haven't made enough sauce, add more stock and thicken it with a beurre manié (see opposite) if need be.

---

* Always use the biggest pan you own.

* Make sure the fruit you use is really ripe.

* Be really careful when cooking jam as hot sugar scalds.

* Bottle your jam or chutney when still hot.

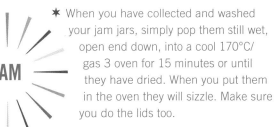

* When you have collected and washed your jam jars, simply pop them still wet, open end down, into a cool 170°C/gas 3 oven for 15 minutes or until they have dried. When you put them in the oven they will sizzle. Make sure you do the lids too.

Traditional GRAVY

Not one of my friends makes their own gravy and I don't know why. We seem to have embraced the Bisto philosophy a bit too much and lost an easy skill in the process. The thing with those gravy granules is that they are vegetarian, meaning they have no meatiness to them and all of their 'meaty' flavour comes from enhancers. They are over-thickened, grainy and, frankly, no match for the real thing. Real gravy is pure and has a strong, natural meaty flavour; not too thin or too thick, it has a good, slightly syrupy consistency.

Serves 4
Preparation time 5 minutes
Cooking time 15 minutes

1 onion, peeled and sliced
4 garlic cloves, peeled
30g plain flour
275ml stock, preferably fresh, of course, but made up from a good cube or liquid is OK too (made from whichever meat you're cooking; see page 246-7 for my stock recipes)
sea salt and freshly ground black pepper

Remove the meat from the roasting tray and set it aside to rest while you make the gravy. Pour off all but 2 tablespoons of fat from the pan, reserving any pan juices and putting them to one side. If there is not enough fat, add some vegetable oil to make up the difference.

Add the onion and whole garlic cloves to the pan and fry for 5 minutes, scraping the sediment from the bottom as you go.

Stir in the flour and cook over a medium heat for a minute. Add the stock bit by bit until combined, whisking as you go. Put back on the heat and cook slowly for 10 minutes. Season to taste, strain and serve in a gravy jug.

A rich wine gravy: Add a small glass of wine to the pan and reduce it by half before adding the stock – I'd use white wine for chicken and pork, red wine for lamb and beef.

A rich, sweet gravy: Add a tablespoon of redcurrant jelly to the gravy while it's cooking for a sweeter taste. This is particularly good with lamb or game.

Tarragon gravy: Add a handful of fresh tarragon, which is really good with chicken.

Onion gravy: Slow-cook 2 peeeled and finely sliced onions in the oil from the meat until they are golden-brown. Continue as for the gravy recipe above, but do not strain – just serve as is. Great with sausages.

Mint gravy: Add a tablespoon of mint jelly to lamb gravy for added zing.

Classic WHITE SAUCE

Once you have mastered the knack of making a simple white sauce you can embark on all sorts of recipes. Cheese, parsley, onion and béchamel sauces are all from this family, as are the soufflé and some custards. These sauces are so easy to make from store-cupboard ingredients and can transform the most boring of meals into something truly terrific.

Serves 4
Preparation time 5 minutes
Cooking time 15 minutes

20g butter
20g plain flour
275ml milk
sea salt and freshly ground black pepper

Melt the butter in a small pan. Add the flour and stir over a low heat for 1 minute until the roux foams.

Remove from the heat and gradually add the milk, whisking as you go: the sauce will thicken almost straight away, but the more milk you add, the thinner the sauce will become. (If you don't add the milk very slowly the sauce will become lumpy.)

Place the pan back on the heat and stir until boiling. Boil for 2 minutes, but continue to stir so the sauce doesn't catch on the bottom of the pan. Season with salt and pepper.

WHY NOT TRY?

Béchamel sauce: Infuse the cold milk for 30 minutes with whole cloves, a halved onion, peppercorns, bay leaves and parsley stalks, then strain them out and use the milk to make a rich, full-flavoured sauce. For the perfect topping when it comes to lasagne or moussaka, add a ball of diced buffalo mozzarella and a handful of grated Parmesan.

Cheese sauce: Add 1 teaspoon of Dijon mustard, a handful of Cheddar and a sprinkling of Parmesan once you put the pan back on the heat. Melt slowly for a rich cheese sauce. Great for cauliflower cheese or macaroni.

Parsley sauce: Add a handful of chopped parsley and a pinch of paprika once you put the pan back on the heat for a soothing sauce. Perfect in a fish pie.

Onion sauce: Add 2 sweated, finely chopped onions in with the butter to make an old-fashioned sauce that's lovely with sausages or lamb.

A velvety VELOUTÉ

This is a lesser-known sauce but it's the base of many a good pie. Rather than a white sauce, why not try a velouté for your chicken or fish pies? The inclusion of stock gives it added flavour and the cream adds a luxurious velvety softness … the ultimate indulgence in sauces.

Melt the butter in a small pan. Add the flour and stir over a low heat for 1 minute until the roux foams.

Remove from the heat and add the stock, bit by bit, whisking as you go. It will thicken almost straight away, but the more stock you add, the thinner the sauce will become. (If you don't add the stock very slowly it will become lumpy.)

Place the pan back on the heat and stir until boiling. Boil for 2 minutes, but continue to stir so the sauce doesn't catch on the bottom of the pan.

Add the cream and lemon juice and season with salt and pepper.

Serves 4
Preparation time 5 minutes
Cooking time 5 minutes

20g butter
20g plain flour
275ml stock, preferably fresh of course but made up from a good cube or liquid is OK too (made from whichever meat you're cooking; see page 246-7 for my stock recipes)
2 tablespoons double cream
a squeeze of fresh lemon juice
sea salt and freshly ground black pepper

Tarragon velouté: Use chicken stock and chopped tarragon as the perfect base for a chicken pie.

Mushroom velouté: Add a dash of mushroom ketchup and sautéd sliced mushrooms for a delicious sauce to pour over chicken or fish.

Wine velouté: Add a splash of white wine to the pan and let the alcohol burn off before adding the stock.

Simple TOMATO SAUCE

Whether for pasta, pizza, meat, chicken or fish, having a good tomato sauce recipe under your belt is essential. And, trust me, you'll be hard pushed to find a way not to use it! I like it simply stirred into spaghetti for those nights when I am so pooped I cannot be bothered to cook. You just whack it on, let it bubble away and hey presto – a scrumptious stress-free supper!

Serves 4
Preparation time 5 minutes
Cooking time 50 minutes

1 tablespoon olive oil
1 onion, peeled and finely chopped
3 garlic cloves, peeled and finely chopped
2 x 400g tins of chopped tomatoes
1 tablespoon red wine vinegar
1 bay leaf
1 tablespoon tomato purée
sea salt and freshly ground black pepper
a pinch of sugar
1 tablespoon torn fresh basil leaves

Heat the oil in a large pan. Add the onion and gently sauté for 0 minutes, or until soft. Add the garlic and fry for a further minute.

Pour in the tomatoes, then add the vinegar, bay leaf, tomato purée, salt and pepper to taste and sugar. Cook, covered, over a low heat for 40 minutes, until the sauce is rich and has begun to thicken slightly.

Stir in the basil and adjust the seasoning if necessary. Remove the bay leaf before serving.

SEX IT UP!

Puttanesca: Add 4 anchovies and 1 chopped red chilli when frying the onion, and finish with black olives at the end.

Provençal: A bouquet garni, white wine and stock with the tomatoes make this rich sauce great for casseroles.

Spicy Spanish sauce: A pinch of saffron, a pinch of dried chilli, a splash of wine and roasted red peppers (added with the tomatoes) make a delicious sauce to serve with potatoes or pour over chicken.

Pizzaiola: Add a tablespoon of chopped oregano at the end of cooking and blend to make a great sauce for pizza.

Hollandaise SAUCE

There is so much fear out there surrounding foody skills such as making hollandaise or béarnaise sauce, but they are actually incredibly easy. The trick is to let the butter stream really, really slowly into the food mixer in order to get a nice thick, glossy sauce. It's all about patience, but it's wonderful watching your sauce emulsify. It doesn't keep very well, so you do have to make it to order.

Serves 4
Preparation time 5 minutes
Cooking time 10 minutes

For the reduction
1 shallot, peeled and finely chopped
6 tablespoons white wine vinegar
3 black peppercorns
1 bay leaf
2 blades of mace

For the sauce
4 free-range egg yolks
a pinch of sea salt
225g hot melted butter
a squeeze of lemon juice

To make the reduction, place all the ingredients in a small pan and bring to the boil. Keep boiling to reduce the amount of liquid until you have 2 tablespoons left, then strain into a cold bowl.

Whiz the egg yolks in a food processor with a pinch of salt. Pour in half the reduction.

Add the butter very, very slowly – 1 teaspoon at a time – until half of it has been used up (the sauce should be fairly thick at this point). Pour in the rest of the butter in a fine stream until all has combined. Alternatively you can make the sauce by hand, beating the ingredients together with a balloon or electric whisk, in a Pyrex bowl set over a bain-marie.

Season with salt, lemon juice and remaining reduction if the sauce needs it.

Béarnaise sauce: Add chopped tarragon and chervil to your finished hollandaise sauce – an absolute classic with steak.

Beurre BLANC

You don't see beurre blanc on many menus these days, which is a shame because it's delicious. So I'm going on a one-woman mission to get everyone eating it. It's a fantastic accompaniment to fish, chicken and vegetables and it's superb as a base, as it can be infused with all sorts of wonderful flavours. For example, pan-fried salmon with grapefruit beurre blanc is an absolute gem.

Serves 4
Preparation time 5 minutes
Cooking time 10 minutes

1 tablespoon finely chopped shallot
3 tablespoons white wine vinegar
225g unsalted butter, chopped into cubes
a squeeze of fresh lemon juice
sea salt and freshly ground black pepper

Place the shallot, vinegar and 3 tablespoons of water in a shallow pan. Bring to the boil then keep boiling to reduce until there are 2 tablespoons of liquid left. Strain the liquid and pour back into the pan.

Lower the heat and gradually whisk in the butter cube by cube. This process should take 3–5 minutes, by which time you should have a pale, creamy sauce.

Season with salt, pepper and lemon juice.

Orange beurre blanc: Add some orange zest and juice at the end of cooking. Delicious with chicken or fish.

Grapefruit beurre blanc: Add some grapefruit zest and juice at the end of cooking. Spot on with steamed white fish or pan-fried salmon.

Saffron beurre blanc: Add a splash of white wine to the reduction in place of the water, plus a pinch of saffron. Finish with 2 tablespoons cream. Superb with shellfish.

Mayonnaise

Can you imagine a sandwich without mayonnaise, or fresh prawns without a dollop of it on top? You can't compare jarred and fresh mayonnaise, especially when you're eating it with seafood – the fresh version wins every time. The trick to a good mayo, as with butter sauces, is dribbling the oil in very, very slowly to produce a mayonnaise with just the right amount of wobble!

Makes 275ml
Preparation time 10 minutes

2 free-range egg yolks
sea salt and freshly ground black pepper
1 teaspoon Dijon mustard
¼ teaspoon white wine vinegar
150ml olive oil
150ml vegetable oil

Whiz the egg yolks together in a food processor with a pinch of salt and pepper, the mustard and the vinegar.

Pour the two oils into a jug together and then, very, very slowly add to the egg-yolk mixture, 1 teaspoon at a time, until half of it has been used up (the sauce should be fairly thick at this point). Pour in the rest of the oil in a fine stream until combined. The mayonnaise should be thick and wobbly. Add a dash more vinegar and season to taste.

Marie Rose sauce: For the classic prawn cocktail sauce, add 2 tablespoons of ketchup, 1 tablespoon of tomato purée, 1 teaspoon of horseradish sauce, a few dashes of Tabasco, a few dashes of Worcestershire sauce and a squeeze of lemon juice.

Aioli: Add 1–3 crushed garlic cloves at the end. I find chips naked without it!

Quince aioli: Whisk in 2 tablespoons of melted quince jam or membrillo paste at the start of the mayonnaise-making process. Amazing with freshly grilled chorizo, roasted pepper and rocket sandwiches.

Tartare sauce: Add 1 tablespoon of chopped gherkins, 1 tablespoon of chopped capers, 2 chopped shallots, 1 tablespoon of chopped fresh parsley, 1 teaspoon chopped fresh dill and a squeeze of lemon juice at the end for the best accompaniment to battered or breaded fish.

Rouille: Add 1–2 crushed garlic cloves, 1 chopped red chilli and a puréed roasted red pepper at the end. Serve on French bread with a fish soup like bouillabaisse. Yum.

Coronation sauce: Add 1 tablespoon of curry powder, 2 tablespoons of mango chutney and 2 tablespoons of plain yoghurt at the end. Pour over poached chicken and serve with lots of fresh watercress.

White CHICKEN STOCK

My mum used to make her chicken stock with the leftover carcasses from our Sunday roast and, while this method does produce a marvellous stock, for purity and clarity the best results come from using fresh carcasses. If you have trouble finding raw chicken carcasses, ask your butcher for some skinned chicken wings. Stock-making is a slow process, but I find it really therapeutic and am a massive advocate of it as it means you are using every last morsel of an animal. Chicken stock freezes brilliantly, and if you invest in lots of 400ml Tupperware containers, you will have it to hand whenever you need it. Use your fresh chicken stock in brothy or puréed soups, stews, gravies and wherever else they are called for!

Makes 1.5 litres
Preparation time 10 minutes
Cooking time 3 hours, 15 minutes

3 roast chicken carcasses (after each roast remember to pop the carcass into a bag and freeze it until you have enough saved up), or 3–4 raw chicken carcasses (from your butcher)
2 onions, peeled and quartered
1 garlic bulb, halved
2 carrots, peeled and chopped into 3 pieces
2 leeks, chopped into 3 pieces
a few fresh herbs if you have them lying around, such as parsley stalks and sprigs of thyme
1 bay leaf
8 black peppercorns

Place all the ingredients in a large, deep cooking pot and cover with cold water. Slowly bring to the boil. As it begins to boil, scum will rise to the surface. With a large spoon or a small ladle skim this off, along with any fat. When the stock has reaching boiling point, turn the heat down and let it gently simmer away for 3 hours (it's important to make sure it doesn't boil at this stage, or the bubbles will knock away at the proteins and make the stock cloudy). While it's simmering, keep skimming the top of the stock as it cooks, mainly for the first 30 minutes' cooking time.

As the stock cooks it will begin to reduce – if the water level falls below the contents of the pot, add a bit more cold water (this will reveal any scum hiding at the bottom of the pan).

When the 3 hours are up, place a fine sieve over a large pan or mixing bowl and pour the stock through, collecting all the flavoursome juices. If you taste the stock at this stage it may not have much flavour, so you need to reduce the liquid by boiling it slowly in order for the flavours to be condensed. To do this, put it back on the hob and bring it to the boil. As it reduces, taste it every so often and when you have the right intensity of chickenyness, season slightly with salt to bring out more flavour. Either use the stock straight away or let it cool and transfer it to the fridge. A good chicken stock will have a really chickeny essence to it and on refrigeration will turn to jelly.

Dark chicken stock: For a richer stock that's great with gravies and meat stews, roast the veggies and chicken carcasses in a really hot oven for 30 minutes, or until they have become golden and caramelized (be careful not to burn them, though, as this charred flavour will transfer to the stock). Then cook the stock as above.

Beef or veal stock: Normally served as a dark stock. Swap the chicken carcasses for 2kg of beef or veal shin bones and cook in the same way as the dark chicken stock. You will need to cook this for 3–4 hours, though. Veal stock is the best to use when making meat gravies, as it will give you that really restauranty flavour.

Fish stock: Swap the chicken carcasses for the carcasses (not heads) of 3 largish white fish or 1kg fish bones. Salmon or tuna make horrid stock, so I would go for sea bass, halibut, haddock and the like. Cook in the same way as the white chicken stock, but only cook for 20 minutes before straining. There is a fine line when making fish stock where it becomes quite rancid if cooked for too long.

Veggie stock: Leave out the chicken carcasses and double the amount of vegetables in the white chicken stock recipe, adding 2 parsnips and some of the outer leaves of a cabbage. Cover with cold water and cook gently for 20 minutes. As with fish stock, vegetable stock needs to be scented and can taste and smell too strong if cooked for too long – think of the stewed veg you used to get at school!

Raspberry COULIS

Makes enough for 6–8 people
400g raspberries
2 tablespoons icing sugar
a squeeze of lemon juice

Place the raspberries, sugar and lemon juice in a blender and whiz until smooth. Tease through a fine sieve and taste. It may need a little more lemon or sugar. Serve over ice cream or with meringues.

Rich CHOCOLATE SAUCE

Makes enough for 6–8 people
200g dark chocolate
500ml double cream
2 tablespoons honey

Place the chocolate, cream and honey in a small pan and melt gently over a low heat. The sauce will become luscious, thick and shiny once it's ready. Use hot or cold.

Blond MOCHA SAUCE

Makes enough for 6–8 people
225g white chocolate
1 vanilla pod, seeds scraped out
500ml double cream
2½ teaspoons instant espresso powder (make sure it's the powder not the grains)

Place the white chocolate, vanilla, cream and espresso powder in a small pan and melt gently over a low heat. Whisk together to make sure the coffee is distributed evenly. It will thicken and go glossy on whipping gently. Use hot or cold over ice cream.

Salted BUTTERSCOTCH SAUCE

Makes enough for 6–8 people
100g light muscovado sugar
100g butter
150ml double cream
1 tablespoon golden syrup
½ teaspoon sea salt

Place all the ingredients in a pan and melt together gently until the sugar has dissolved. Bring to the boil for 3–4 minutes, or until the sauce has darkened a little and gone syrupy and shiny. Serve poured over ice cream.

Custard

I'm going to be the first to admit that I am a huge fan of Bird's Custard in all its bright yellow glory, but making custard from scratch is super-delicious and such an achievement. Just be really gentle with the heat to avoid the eggs scrambling and the second you think it's thick enough, whip it off the heat and strain it. Needless to say, scrummy on any baked or steamed pudding and with stewed fruit.

Makes enough for 6–8 people to accompany a pudding

1 vanilla pod or 1 teaspoon vanilla extract
500ml double cream
5 egg yolks
1 whole egg
85g caster sugar

Scrape the seeds from 1 vanilla pod and put both seeds and pod into a pan with the cream. Bring to the boil slowly, and take off the heat once the edge starts to fizz with bubbles.

In a bowl, whisk 5 egg yolks and the whole egg with the caster sugar until pale and thick. Whisk in the vanilla-infused milk, then strain into a clean pan and put back on a lowish heat, stirring continuously, until the custard thickens.

Passion FRUIT CURD

As you would need about a million passion fruit to make this in bulk, it's only really possible to make small quantities, but this fact makes the curd all the more special.

Makes 1–2 jam jars
Preparation time 15 minutes
Cooking time 10 minutes

2 large free-range eggs
125ml passion fruit juice (about 12 passion
   fruits, pulped and sieved)
80g caster sugar
60g softened unsalted butter

Place the eggs, passion fruit juice and sugar in a bowl over a pan of simmering water. Stir continuously with a wooden spoon for 8 minutes or until thickened. Remove from the heat and whisk in the butter. Pop into sterilised jam jars and, when cool, refrigerate. Keep for up to 6 weeks – not that you'll be able to …

WHY NOT TRY?

Serve it with warm scones or, even better, with meringues and cream à la Eton mess!

Strawberry & TARRAGON JAM

Tarragon's aniseed flavour adds depth to strawberry jam and gives it a more grown-up taste. It's incredible with homemade scones and clotted cream, accompanied by a glass of floral green tea. Use this jam recipe as a guide to making other varieties, bearing in mind that different fruit will require different cooking times.

The day before you wish to make the jam, hull and halve the strawberries and place them in a large bowl with 500g of the sugar. Turn carefully to mix and coat well, then cover with clingfilm and place in the fridge overnight.

Place a freezerproof saucer in the freezer. Pour the strawberries and any residual sugary juices into a very large pan or preserving pan, remembering that the mixture will rise as it boils. Add the remaining 500g of sugar and the lemon juice. Stir over a gentle heat until the sugar has completely dissolved. Bring the strawberries up to the boil, then boil hard for 10 minutes, by which time the jam may have reached setting point.

To test this, remove the pan from the heat. Take the saucer from the freezer and place a drop of jam on it. After a few seconds, push the jam gently with your finger. If the surface wrinkles, it has reached setting point and is ready. If it slides about as a liquid, the pan should be returned to the heat and the jam boiled for a further 2 minutes before testing again. Continue to do this every 10 minutes until the jam reaches setting point, which could take up to 30 minutes.

When setting point has been reached, turn off the heat. Stir in the butter and the sprig of tarragon and, using a large slotted spoon, remove any scum that rises to the surface of the jam. Let the jam cool and thicken in the pan for 10 minutes (this will also prevent the strawberries from sinking to the bottom of the jars).

Stir the jam, then ladle it into sterilised jars. Use a jam funnel, if you have one, to avoid spilling too much. Cover the top surface of the jam in each jar with a waxed paper disc cut to size – it should cover the entire surface of the jam. Press the disc down to create a complete seal. Fasten with a lid while still hot, label and store in a cool, dark cupboard for up to a year.

Makes 4–6 jars
Preparation time 20 minutes
Macerating time overnight
Cooking time 40 minutes

1kg strawberries
1kg jam sugar or golden granulated sugar
juice of ½ lemon
a small knob of butter
a sprig of fresh tarragon

WHY
NOT
TRY?

Blackberry and rosemary jam: Swap the strawberries for the same quantity of blackberries and the tarragon for 2 stalks of rosemary and make the recipe in the exact same way.

Christmas CHUTNEY

This might be called Christmas chutney, but it is one of those things that is so damn good it's great at any time. The Christmassy element comes from the spices and the jammy sweetness that the apricots provide. Like a Christmas pudding, I would make a batch a couple of months in advance so that it has time to mature and get really full-bodied, ready for when you want to slather it all over your Boxing Day turkey and ham sandwiches!

Makes 4–6 jars
Preparation time 20 minutes
Cooking time 1 hour

4 oranges, unpeeled and finely chopped
1.5kg apricots, stoned and quartered
4 onions, thinly sliced
450g golden caster sugar
1 teaspoon salt
½ teaspoon ground cloves
1 teaspoon ground black pepper
½ teaspoon chilli flakes
½ teaspoon ground mace
1 teaspoon curry powder
1 tablespoon mustard seeds
1 teaspoon turmeric
1 litre cider vinegar

Place all the ingredients into a large stock pot or the biggest saucepan you have.

Bring to the boil, then reduce the heat and simmer for 1 hour until thick, stirring occasionally, especially nearer the end of cooking time, to make sure it does not scorch. It may take a little longer than an hour – what you're looking for is a jammy chutney consistency.

Pour into sterilised jam or kilner jars, top each one with a piece of waxed paper and seal tightly. Let the chutney cool in the jars and store in a cool dark cupboard for up to a year. I would leave it to mature and develop its flavour for at least a month before eating, though it's obviously fine to eat straight away, once cool.

Spiced RED ONION JAM

A jar of onion jam is great with so many things, a cheeseboard, a steak sandwich or hamburger would be pointless without it. It is really therapeutic to prepare, and a couple of spoonfuls of it added to your regular gravy will give you a fab cheats' onion gravy too!

Makes 4–6 jars
Preparation time 10 minutes
Cooking time 1 hour

2 tablespoons olive oil
1.5kg red onions, peeled and thinly sliced
100g golden caster sugar
½ teaspoon chilli flakes
a few sprigs of fresh thyme, leaves picked
300ml red wine vinegar
1 glass of red wine
½ glass of port

Heat the oil in a large, heavy-based pan and cook the onions very slowly over a low heat for 30 minutes, or until they have softened so much that they have become caramelised. Add the sugar, chilli flakes and thyme and cook for a further 10 minutes.

Pour over the vinegar, red wine and port and simmer, uncovered, for 20 minutes, stirring every so often, until the onions are a deep red colour and there is only a small pool of liquid floating around the bottom of the pan. To test, draw a wooden spoon through the jam – a path should clear before filling again with syrupy juices.

Leave the onions to cool in the pan, then fill sterilised jars with the mixture. It can be eaten straight away, but tastes great when it has had a couple of weeks to mature. Store in a cool dark cupboard for up to a year.

Acknowledgements

To begin with, I would like to thank Richard Cable for seeing something in me all those moons ago and giving me the opportunity to write this book. Next, Louisa Joyner, who came in, saved the day and shook us all up. You have been the most amazing sounding board, not just about this book but about everything. You would make the most incredible agony aunt! Sorry about all my whinging and thank you for your patience. Sophia Brown, for all of your hard work, faith and honesty with regards to my recipes. Like you, I still feel that the rosemary-infused millionaire's shortbread is revolutionary. To David Loftus for your incredible photographs and having tons of fun shooting the recipes – you know how much I adore you. To Chris Terry for our show-stopping cover shot and frankly being one of the coolest guys in the universe! To Lucy Stephens, our cover rocks. Thank you for its beautiful design. Then to Vickie Boff, for listening to moan after moan from me – it's a wonder you haven't gone potty. I hope that you know how much I value you and everything you have done for me!

I have to give a jumbo shout-out to my beautiful mother Maria, who has probably been bugged about every single recipe in this book. I owe all my love of food to you and thank you for giving us such a healthy outlook on eating and embracing food like it's a part of us. You are and will always remain my biggest inspiration. To my father Iain, who is sadly no longer with us – I miss you every day and wish you could have seen all this. To Dean, for being honest with me about everything during our mammoth tasting sessions and going along with this journey with me from the start. Boy, how things have changed. Without a doubt, I would not have been able to do any of this without you. I feel that whatever I gain you deserve credit for it too. I love you beyond words and can't wait to see what the future will bring us.

To Cora and Heni, for being my best friends as well as sisters. You both keep me grounded (even if it is because I know you guys have so much on me!!!) Time spent with you both, as well as Matt and Edie, has been a sanctuary away from the craziness that is my life. My step-mum Debra – you do realise this has everything to do with you?! I can't thank you enough for introducing me to Nick Perren (who I also owe a HUGE shout-out to), who got the whole ball rolling. To Jonathan Shalit, I cannot thank you enough for turning things round for me and Severine Berman – you are like an angel, you work so damn hard but still do it with that cheeky grin. You are masters at what you do. Liz Matthews, Tim and Joel – I don't really know where to start. Since working with you, everything has gained momentum and I feel like I owe so much to you all and your amazing skills. Thank you for encouraging me to stay true to myself, in a world where everyone is trying to mould me. Sheila Crowley – ultimately this book is down to you. When you took me under your wing way back when, all this was just a pipe dream, but you made it happen. I am so grateful.

A few people that cannot go unmentioned are Jo McGrath, for all your support, Martin Frizell, Liz Belton, Annie Lee, Sarah Barlow, Laura Hatton, Carolyn Thorne, Abbey Dempsey, Rich Carr, Bella Crane, Falcon, Kitchen Aid, Le Creuset, Emma Justice and Company magazine and finally my bessie mate Martha. Bloody love you. xx

★ ☆ Index ☆ ★